Classic
Woodworking
Projects

Handyman Club Library™

Handyman Club of America
Minnetonka, Minnesota

Classic Woodworking Projects

Printed in 2010.

CREDITS

Tom Carpenter
Creative Director

Dan Cary
Photo Production Coordinator

Chris Marshall
Editorial Coordinator

Kam Ghaffari, Mark Johanson
Writers

Marti Naughton
Series Design, Art Direction and Production

Kim Bailey
Lead Photographer

Tad Saddoris
Photography

Tom Deveny, Bob Ginn, Jon Hegge, John Nadeau
Project Builders

Steve Anderson
Contributing Writer

Dan Cary, Tom Deveny, Mark Johanson, Bruce Kieffer, Chris Marshall
Project Designers

Craig Claeys, Bill Nelson, Gina Seeling
Contributing Design and Illustration

ISBN 10: 1-58159-007-5
ISBN 13: 978-1-58159-007-4
© 1998 Handyman Club of America
12 13 / 13 12 11 10

Handyman Club of America
12301 Whitewater Drive
Minnetonka, Minnesota 55343
www.handymanclub.com

Contents

Garden Bench (150)

Toy Chest (66)

Tile-top Coffee Table (142)

Magazine Rack (10)

Adirondack Chair (18)

Three-legged Stool (122)

Picnic Table & Benches (58)

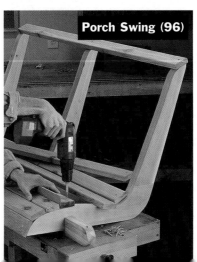
Porch Swing (96)

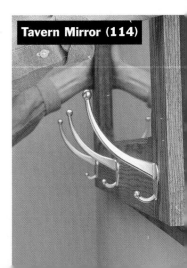
Tavern Mirror (114)

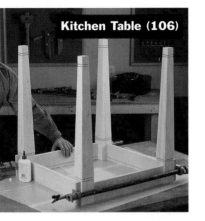
Misson Rocker (76)

Plant Stand (134)

Kitchen Table (106)

Oak Cabinets (36)

Colonial Step Stool (50)

Formal Bookcase (88)

Workbench (28)

Introduction

Even in woodworking, fashions come and fashions go. Today's popular designs can quickly become tomorrow's flea market specials. But some designs are different. They withstand the test of time and grow old without apology. These are the classic woodworking designs, and you'll find 16 of the best in this new volume of woodworking plans, created exclusively for the Members of the Handyman Club of America.

From backyard standards to fine furniture, all of the projects featured in this book have a few important characteristics in common: they're simple and elegant, not flashy; they're useful and practical, not strictly for show; and they're designed so they can be built by just about anyone with a basic woodworking shop and a little experience and patience.

Each project in this book is presented with a complete cutting list, a shopping list, a detailed plan drawing, 10 or more beautiful color photographs of the project as it's being built, and straightforward step-by-step instructions. Before jumping right into the woodworking projects, we've pulled together some information on the next few pages highlighting a few basic techniques that you'll find repeated throughout this book.

BUYING LUMBER

If you've never purchased hardwood at a traditional lumber yard before, learn the basics of buying wood. Knowing up-front how much (and what size) stock to buy for your project will save time, money and aggravation.

Unlike construction grade lumber, hardwood and better quality softwoods are sold by the *board foot*. A board foot is equal to one running (lineal) foot of a board that's 12 in. wide and 1 in. thick. To calculate precisely how many board feet of material you'll need for your project, multiply the length by the width by the thickness (expressed in inches) then divide that number by 144. You can make a quick and easy estimate by simply figuring out how many lineal feet of the stock you want to buy will equal one board foot.

But there's more to buying lumber than simply estimating board feet. Before you start a project, find out what dimensions your local supplier has the species available in and draw cutting diagrams for your project parts, as you would with plywood. Also, be aware that even lumber that's been planed on both sides at the mill will likely require additional planing, so you should buy wood that's at least ¼ in. thicker than the planned thickness of your project part. Hardwood is normally sold in random widths, so don't go to the lumber yard expecting to find a walnut 2 × 4.

1×6: 2 lineal ft. = 1 board ft.

2×6: 1 lineal ft. = 1 board ft.

4×4: 9 lineal in. = 1 board ft.

STEP 1: Run lumber through a thickness planer to create at least one smooth face. Flatten badly warped stock on a jointer first—planing won't flatten warps.

STEP 2: Plane one edge on a jointer until it's perfectly flat. Be sure that the jointer fence is square to the table and a planed face is against the jointer fence.

STEP 3: Rip the stock to width on the table saw. The jointed edge should ride against the saw fence with a planed face on the saw table. The stock is now square.

SQUARING STOCK

Flat, square lumber is essential to virtually all woodworking. Without it, joints cannot be drawn tightly together, workpieces won't line up, and doors and drawers will not operate properly. To be square means that each face of a workpiece is at a right angle to adjacent faces. Squaring stock involves planing one or more faces of a board, then flattening an edge so it forms a right angle to the planed face. Some lumber comes factory-planed and square from the mill. If you buy your lumber rough-sawn, however, use the three-step process shown above to square your stock. Regardless of the initial shape of your lumber, be sure to check all stock for square with a try square before using it.

EDGE-GLUING

Woodworking projects often require solid-wood panels wider than the width of available single boards. You could opt to use a piece of plywood and wrap it with wood edge-banding, but it's relatively easy to glue edge-jointed boards into a solid-wood panel of just about any size you need.

Select boards of consistent grain pattern and color and flatten their edges on a jointer. Arrange them so that the growth rings alternate. You can then glue and clamp the boards without further joint support, or use joint alignment aids, such as biscuits, as we show at right.

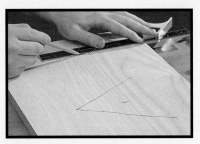

STEP 1: Arrange edge-jointed boards into a panel and draw a "V" across all panel joints. Mark short reference lines every 8-10 in. for biscuits or dowels.

STEP 2: Cut biscuit slots or dowel joints at each reference line.

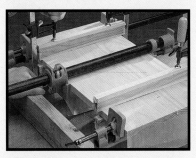

STEP 3: Apply glue to the biscuits or dowels and along one board edge. Press the boards together.

STEP 4: Clamp the panel together, alternating clamps above and below. Tighten clamps just enough to close the joints.

Featured Skill

MAKING DOWEL JOINTS

A quick look through this book will reveal that dowel joints can be found in a majority of the projects. And there's a good reason for that: dowel joints are strong, versatile, they don't require expensive equipment, and they're easy to make. In fact, a doweling jig like the one shown below can be used to make

dowel joints that are practically foolproof (and these jigs are inexpensive and simple to use, to boot). When making dowel joints, you should use premilled, fluted dowels if holding power is an issue. But in many cases, you can get by with pieces of hardwood doweling that you cut yourself.

STEP 1: Butt the mating parts together and draw a straight line across the joint at each planned dowel location. Most dowel joints should have at least two dowels for reinforcement and alignment. For longer joints, space the dowels 8 to 10 in. apart.

STEP 2: Slide the doweling jig over each mating mating edge and align a reference line on the workpiece with the line on the jig that corresponds to the diameter of the dowel being used. Drill holes to the required depth at each dowel location. NOTE: The dowel should be no thicker than half the thickness of the board.

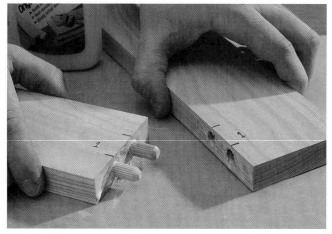

STEP 3: Apply glue into each dowel hole and onto the mating surfaces. Drive dowels into all the dowel holes on one of the boards, then press the board against the mating board to close the joint.

STEP 4: The dowels alone are not enough to ensure a tight joint. Always clamp the boards together, using clamp pads to protect the wood. Locate the heads of the clamp as close as possible to the joints.

Featured Skill

APPLYING A WOOD FINISH

Fine wood finishing is a true art form. But fortunately, even if you don't have the time or interest to develop the art for yourself, today's wood finishing products allow even beginners to produce wood finishes that are more than satisfactory for most woodworking projects. If you're new to wood finishing,

experiment with a few different finishing materials until you find a compatible combination of staining agent and topcoat material that you're comfortable with. Consult with experts for their advice, and always sample a finish on scrap wood before you apply it to the actual project.

STEP 1: Sand all surfaces with progressively finer sandpaper (up to 180-or 220-grit for most hardwood). A random orbit sander works well.

STEP 2: Wipe the surfaces with a tack cloth to remove dust and other debris. Do this no more than 30 minutes before applying the finish.

STEP 3: Apply wood stain (optional) with a staining cloth or a brush. Follow the manufacturer's directions for coverage.

STEP 4: Wipe away excess stain, then reapply if a darker tone is desired. Allow the stain to dry at least overnight before proceeding.

STEP 5: Apply a very thin coat of the clear topcoating product you prefer. The most common finishing mistake is applying overly heavy coats.

STEP 6: Sand the first coat lightly after it dries, using 400-grit sandpaper. Wipe clean, then apply more thin coats (at least three total).

Magazine Rack

Confine the clutter of reading materials into one neat package with this compact and highly attractive magazine rack. Built from solid cherry, this rack design accomplishes an airy, modern feeling without sacrificing the look of fine furniture. And with careful cutting, you can build it from only two cherry boards.

Vital Statistics: Magazine Rack

TYPE: Magazine rack

OVERALL SIZE: 12W by 14H by 12D

MATERIAL: Cherry

JOINERY: Hidden dowel joints

CONSTRUCTION DETAILS:
· Generously spaced slats for contemporary appearance
· Smooth handle profile for comfortable carrying
· Divided compartment promotes organization
· Makes efficient use of materials

FINISHING OPTIONS: Brush on a clear topcoat such as Danish oil (shown). Could leave unfinished to allow tannins in the cherry wood to react with the air and darken the wood naturally.

Building time

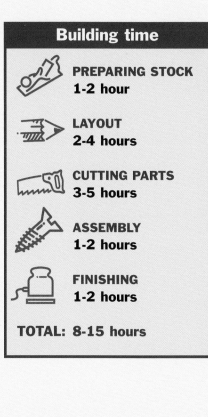

PREPARING STOCK
1-2 hour

LAYOUT
2-4 hours

CUTTING PARTS
3-5 hours

ASSEMBLY
1-2 hours

FINISHING
1-2 hours

TOTAL: 8-15 hours

Tools you'll use

· Jointer
· Table saw
· Planer
· Router with piloted ⅛-in. roundover bit
· Metal rule
· 18-in. or longer bar or pipe clamps (6)
· Jig saw, band saw or scroll saw
· Miter saw (power or hand)
· Portable drill guide
· Doweling jig
· Metal dowel points
· Mallet
· Drill/driver

Shopping list

☐ (1) ⁴⁄₄ × 4+ in. × 8 ft. cherry board
☐ (1) ¾ × 4 in. × 8 ft. cherry board
☐ ¼-in.-dia. hardwood doweling
☐ Wood glue
☐ Finishing materials

Magazine Rack

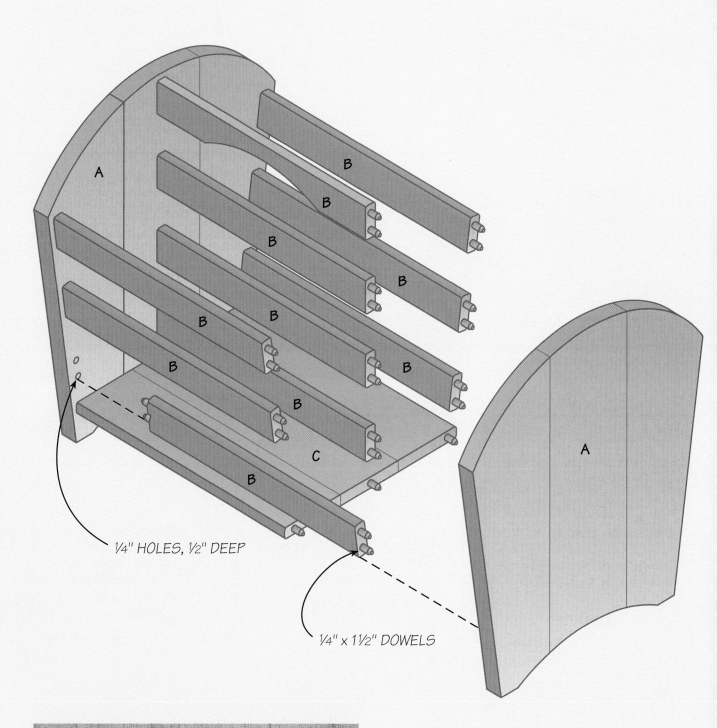

A

B

B

B

B

B

B

B

B

B

B

C

A

¼" HOLES, ½" DEEP

¼" x 1½" DOWELS

Magazine Rack Cutting List			
Part	**No.**	**Size**	**Material**
A. Sides	2	¾ × 12 × 14 in.	Cherry
B. Slats/handle	10	½ × 1½ × 11 in.	"
C. Bottom	1	½ × 9 × 11 in.	"

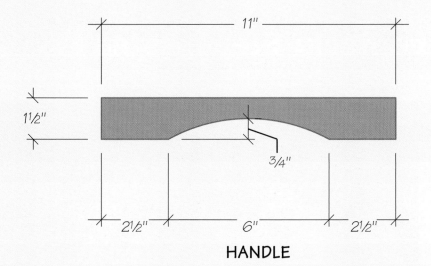

11"

1½"

2½"   6"   2½"

3/4"

HANDLE

¼" HOLES, ½" DEEP IN ENDS AND
1 1/16" DEEP IN RAILS, HANDLE & BOTTOM

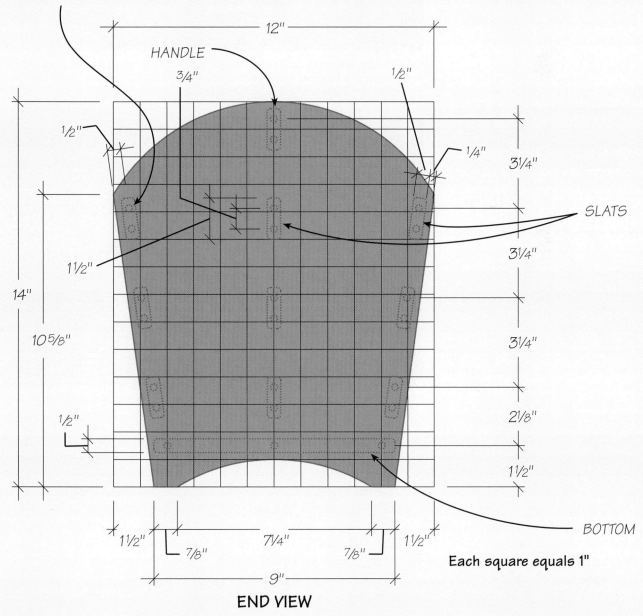

HANDLE

3/4"

12"

½"

½"

1/4"

3¼"

SLATS

3¼"

1½"

3¼"

14"

10⅝"

2⅛"

½"

1½"

1½"   7¼"   7/8"   1½"

7/8"

9"

BOTTOM

Each square equals 1"

END VIEW

CUT THE PARTS TO SIZE

The parts for this magazine rack can all be cut from two 8-ft.-long cherry boards. We edge-glued three strips of ¾-in.(after planing) cherry to make the side panels. The ½-in.-thick bottom panel is also made from edge-glued cherry.

❶ Plane an 8-ft.-long, 4⁄4 cherry board that's at least 4¼ in. wide to ¾ in. thick. Joint one edge of the board, then rip-cut it to 4⅛ in. wide (4¹⁄₁₆ in. is okay). Cross-cut six 15-in.-long sections, and edge-glue them into two panels that are roughly 12 × 15 in. **(See Photo A).** For a good glue joint, joint both edges of the middle board in each glue-up.

❷ Plane a ¾ × 4 in. × 8 ft. board down to ½ in. thick. Rip-cut a 3-ft.-long section from one end of the board, joint one edge, then rip-cut to 3⅛ in. wide. Cut the board into three 12-in.-long sections. Arrange the boards into a panel roughly 9 × 12 in. (joint both edges of the middle board) and glue up the panel to make the bottom of the magazine rack.

❸ On the remaining 5-ft. section of ½-in. stock, joint one edge, then rip-cut the jointed side to 1½ in. wide. Rip-cut the waste strip to 1½ in. wide as well, making sure to run the freshly cut edge against

PHOTO A: Edge-glue panels for the sides and the bottom. As you tighten the clamps, the glue will cause the joints to slide out of alignment, so adjust them as well as you can to keep them lined up. Be sure to use clamping pads to protect the wood.

PHOTO B: Drill small locator holes through the side template, at the centerpoints shown for each dowel location. Use scrap plywood underneath to prevent drill bit tear-out.

your table saw fence. Install a ⅛-in.-radius roundover bit in your router and ease all the edges of both strips. Reserve the strips to cut the rails and the handle.

CUT THE PARTS TO SHAPE

❹ Enlarge the *Grid Drawing* on page 13 to full size by photocopying or by drawing a grid to scale and plotting out the pattern using the drawing as a reference. Secure the full-size drawing to a piece of ¼-in.-thick hardboard or plywood (we used spray adhesive). Cut out the shape along the lines with a band saw, scroll saw or jig saw to create a template. Smooth the sawn edges.

5 Place the template on a piece of scrap plywood to serve as a drilling backup board. Drill small holes (about the diameter of your awl or centerpunch) through the template at the dowel hole center-points shown on the *Grid Drawing* **(See Photo B)**.

6 Cross-cut one end of each glued-up panel for the sides so the end is straight and square to the sides of the panel. Lay the template on each glued-up panel with its bottom edge flush with the squared end. Trace around the template to transfer the cutting shape. Use an awl or centerpunch to mark the dowel-hole centers through the locator holes in the template **(See Photo C)**.

7 Cut out the shapes of the sides using a jig saw, band saw or scroll saw. Cut carefully along the waste sides of the lines **(See Photo D)**. Sand the edges smooth.

8 Drill ¼-in.-dia. × ½-in.-deep dowel holes at the dowel-hole centers marked on each side panel. Use a portable drill guide and a bit stop **(See Photo E)**.

9 Cross-cut the strips of ½ × 1½ in. stock into 10, 11-in.-long strips **(See Photo F)** to make the nine rails and the handle. We used a power miter saw with a stopblock set at 11 in. to speed up the cutting and ensure uniforms lengths.

10 Choose one piece for the handle and draw a contour line for making the handle cutout. The arched cutout starts 2½ in. from each end and is ¾ high at the center (See *Detail Drawing*, page 13). Cut out the arc along the contour line and smooth the cut with a sander or file.

PHOTO C: Center the template on each side panel and outline the shape. Poke an awl or centerpunch through the template holes to mark centerpoints for the dowel holes.

PHOTO D: Cut out the end shapes. We used a jig saw, but you could use a band saw or scroll saw instead. Cut along the waste sides of the cutting lines, then smooth the cuts with a file or by sanding with medium-grit sandpaper.

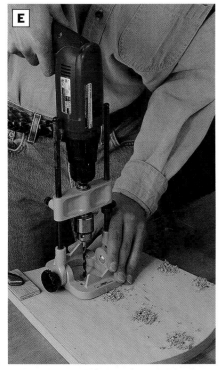

PHOTO E: Drill ½-in-deep dowel holes at the dowel hole centers you marked on each of the two sides with the hardboard template. Use a drill guide to ensure straight holes.

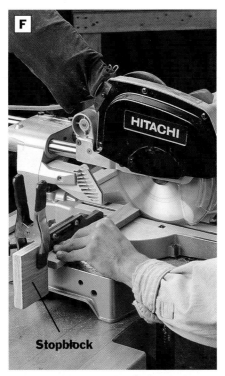

Stopblock

PHOTO F: Clamp a stopblock to the fence of a power miter saw, 11 in. from the edge of the blade, to make uniform cross-cuts when cutting the rails and handle pieces to length.

ASSEMBLE THE MAGAZINE RACK

Assembling the magazine rack can get tricky, since it involves 46 dowel pins (and 92 dowel holes). On the plus side, the scale of the project makes it easy to handle, so assembling the rack before the glue sets should be no problem.

⓫ Start with the bottom panel and drill three ¼-in.-dia. × 1¹⁄₁₆-in.-deep dowel holes in each end. The holes should align with the dowel holes you drilled into the bottoms of the side panels, using the template. To ensure that the holes do align, insert metal dowel points into the holes in the side panels, set the bottom panel in the correct position against the side panel, and press the two workpieces together. The pointed spur at the end of each dowel point will make a clear center-point for a corresponding dowel

PHOTO G: Use a doweling jig to drill centered dowel holes in the ends of the rails and handle. Clamp rails together edge-to-edge to provide more surface area for the jig.

PHOTO H: Glue the dowels in the ends of the handle, the slats, and the bottom into the corresponding dowel holes in one side panel. Then immediately glue dowels into the other end panel and set it onto the upright ends of the parts. Align the dowels into their holes and press the assembly together.

hole in the end of the bottom panel. Use a drill press or a drilling guide to bore the dowel holes. If you use a drilling guide, sandwich each workpiece between scrap boards to provide more support for the guide.

⓬ Drill two ¼-in.-dia. × 1¹⁄₁₆-in.-deep dowel holes in the end of each slat and in each end of the handle. Use a doweling jig to center the holes. Clamp a few parts at a time into your bench vise, aligning the ends straight across. This provides more bearing surface for the jig **(See Photo G).**

⓭ Sand all the parts to 220-grit. Ease all sharp edges except for the ends of the rails and handles.

⓮ Apply glue and lightly tap ¼ × 1½-in. lengths of hardwood doweling into the dowel holes in one end of each cross member (the slats, the bottom and the handle).

⓯ Lay one side of the magazine rack on a worksurface so the dowel holes are facing up. Glue the joints and insert the cross members **(See Photo H).**

⓰ Immediately glue and tap dowels into the holes in the other side panel. Then lay that panel on top of the exposed ends of the cross members, aligning the dowels with the corresponding dowel holes. Once the dowels are aligned, seat them by pressing against the cross members. Clamp the project across its ends, using cauls to spread the clamping pressure **(See Photo I).**

⓱ Touch up any rough surfaces or edges with 220-grit sandpaper. Apply the finish. We brushed on three coats of clear, Danish oil **(See Photo J).**

PHOTO I: Clamp up the rack assembly, using wood cauls to distribute pressure evenly. Use three pairs of bar or pipe clamps.

PHOTO J: Because of all the flat, narrow surfaces that are easy to access, a brush-on finish is a good choice for this magazine rack. We used three coats of Danish oil for an even, satiny finish.

Adirondack Chair

The Adirondack chair has become a fixture in the backyards of America. There are countless variations of the basic design, but all share a few common elements: wide armrests that are usually flared toward the front; slatted backs and seats (although the original Adirondack chairs featured solid backs and seats); a contoured profile at the tops of the back slats; and a sleek, angular, low-to-the-ground undercarriage. The Adirondack chair design shown here is among the simpler plans you'll find published today. It features graceful lines and sturdy construction. And building this chair is not a summer-long project.

Vital Statistics: Adirondack Chair

TYPE: Outdoor chair

OVERALL SIZE: 30½W by 38H by 33½D

MATERIAL: Cedar

JOINERY: Screw-reinforced butt joints

CONSTRUCTION DETAILS:

· 12-in.-radius profile on top of slatted back
· Broad arms
· Seat sloped and contoured for comfort
· Low angle on back legs for characteristic Adirondack look

FINISHING OPTIONS: Clear-coat with UV-resistant clear wood sealant (shown); stain with oil-based redwood or cedar stain for richer wood tones; paint in traditional Adirondack color (hunter green, gray, or white); leave unfinished to fade to natural gray tone.

Building time

PREPARING STOCK
1 hour

LAYOUT
2-4 hours

CUTTING PARTS
3-5 hours

ASSEMBLY
2-4 hours

FINISHING
1-2 hours

TOTAL: 9-16 hours

Tools you'll use

· Surface planer
· Table saw
· Jig saw or scroll saw
· C-clamps
· Spring clamps
· Tape measure
· Combination square/metal rule
· Drill/driver

Shopping list

☐ (2) 1 × 6 in. × 6 ft. cedar boards (nominal)

☐ (3) 1 × 4 in. × 8 ft. cedar boards (nominal)

☐ (5) 1 × 4 in. × 6 ft. cedar boards (nominal)

☐ Galvanized deck screws (2 in., 1¼ in.)

☐ Water-resistant (exterior) wood glue

☐ Finishing materials

Adirondack Chair

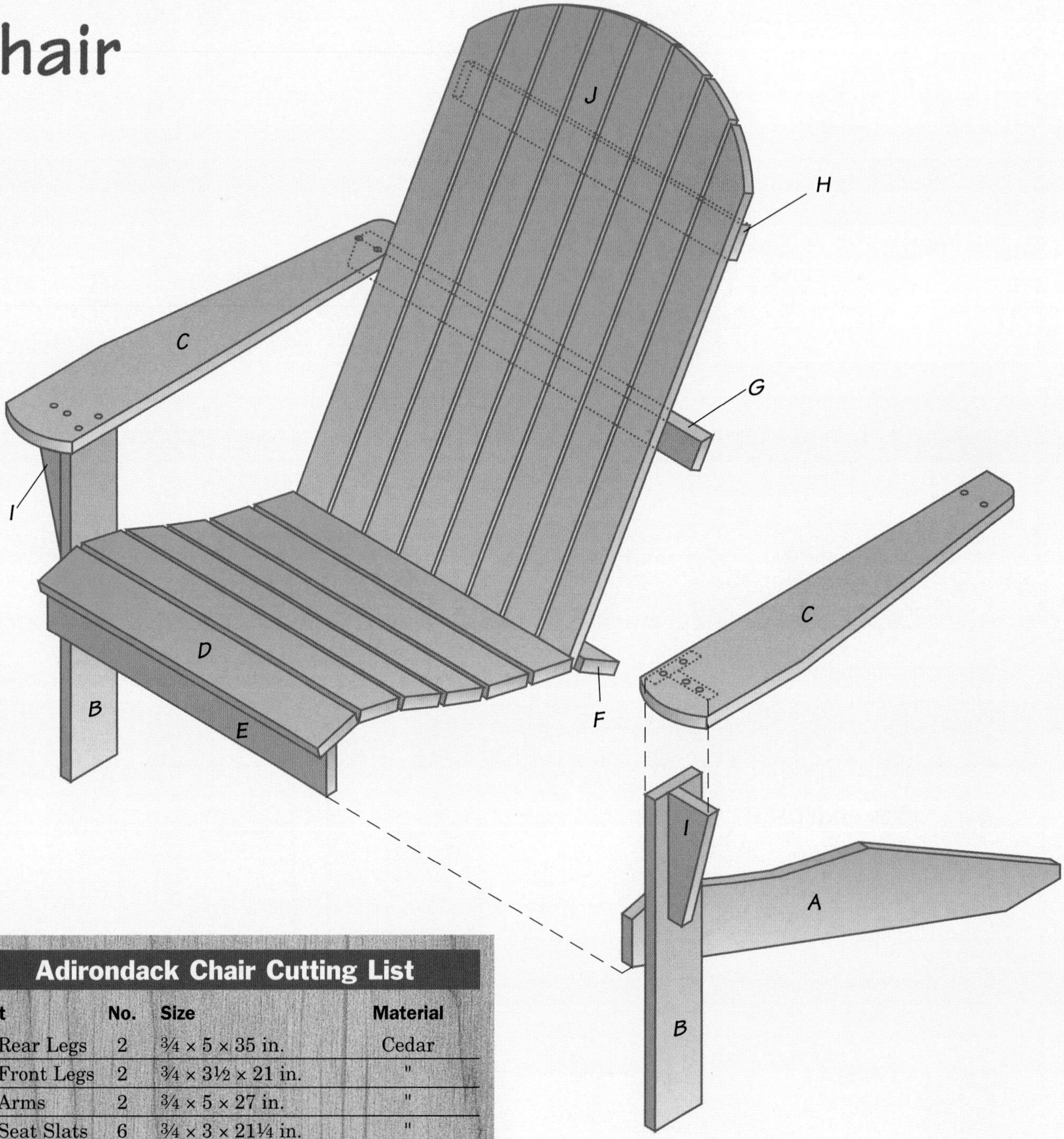

Adirondack Chair Cutting List			
Part	**No.**	**Size**	**Material**
A. Rear Legs	2	¾ × 5 × 35 in.	Cedar
B. Front Legs	2	¾ × 3½ × 21 in.	"
C. Arms	2	¾ × 5 × 27 in.	"
D. Seat Slats	6	¾ × 3 × 21¼ in.	"
E. Front Seat Support	1	¾ × 3 × 21¼ in.	"
F. Lower Back Support	1	¾ × 3 × 21¼ in.	"
G. Center Back Support	1	¾ × 2 × 26 in.	"
H. Upper Back Support	1	¾ × 2 × 20¾ in.	"
I. Arm Supports	2	¾ × 3 × 8 in.	"
J. Back Slats	8	¾ × 2⅜ × 32 in.	"

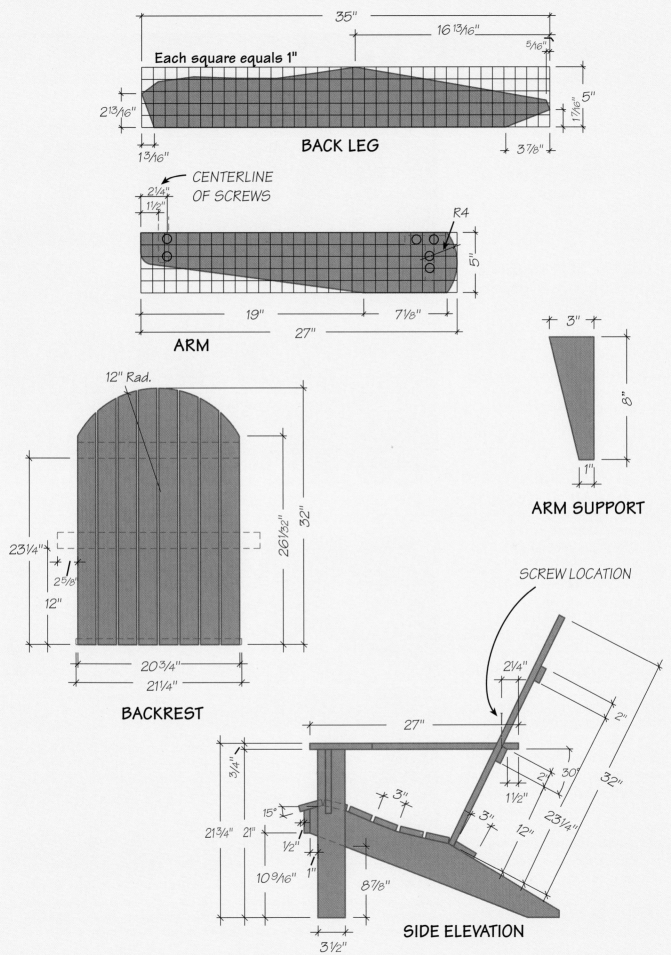

35"

16 13/16"

5/16"

Each square equals 1"

2 13/16"

1 7/16" **5"**

1 3/16"

3 7/8"

BACK LEG

CENTERLINE
OF SCREWS

2 1/4"

1 1/2"

R4

5"

19"

7 1/8"

27"

ARM

3"

8"

1"

ARM SUPPORT

12" Rad.

23 1/4"

2 5/8"

12"

26 3/32"

32"

20 3/4"

21 1/4"

BACKREST

SCREW LOCATION

2 1/4"

2"

27"

2"

30"

32"

1 1/2"

3/4"

15°

3"

3"

23 1/4"

21 3/4" **21"**

1/2"

12"

1"

10 9/16"

8 7/8"

3 1/2"

SIDE ELEVATION

MAKE THE ARMS & BACK LEGS
Contoured arms, legs and slats give the Adirondack chair its distinctive appearance. Carefully recreating the angles shown for these parts is an important step in successfully building your own Adirondack chair. For consistency and control, we made full-size templates for each type of part.

1 Enlarge the grid patterns (page 21) for the back legs and the arms to full size on sturdy paper (you can use a photocopier or a pantograph, or simply draw a scaled grid on the template material and copy the outline using the grid drawing for reference). Attach the template drawing to a scrap piece of ¼-in. hardboard or plywood with spray-on adhesive. Cut out the contours of the shapes with a jig saw, band saw or scroll saw. Follow the lines carefully, cutting along the waste side. Make a relief cut from the outside edge to the line at the sharp inside corner on the back leg, to allow the waste to fall away, or cut from both directions toward the corner. File and sand the edges smooth. Drill small holes the size of a finish nail through the arm template at the screw centerpoints, as shown on the grid pattern.

2 All of the parts for this Adirondack chair were cut from dimen-

PHOTO A: Create templates for the contoured arms and the back legs, using the grid patterns on page 21 as a reference, then transfer the shapes onto prepared cedar stock that has been cut to size.

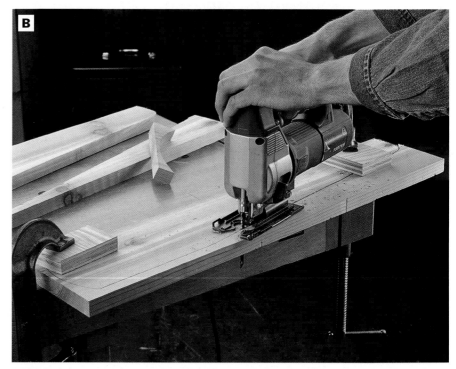

PHOTO B: Cut out the arms and legs along the contoured cutting lines, using a jig saw, band saw or scroll saw. Cut just outside of the cutting lines, then gang-sand the parts down to the lines with a random-orbit sander or a drum sander mounted in your drill press.

sional cedar purchased at a building center. The cedar we purchased was surfaced on one side only (which is typical), so we ran the rough faces through a surface planer to smooth them out and to reduce the stock from 7/8 to 3/4 in. in thickness. To make the arms and legs, cut surfaced stock to the dimensions shown in the *Cutting list* (page 20), then affix the correct template to each piece of stock with double-faced tape. Trace around the template with a pencil **(See Photo A).** Poke a finish nail or scratch awl through the screw centerpoint holes on the arm template to mark screw locations for future reference.

3 Cut out the arms and legs with a jig saw, band saw or scroll saw **(See Photo B).**

CUT THE REMAINING PARTS
4 Cut the two arm supports to 3 in. wide × 8 in. long. Draw a tapered cutting line on each part so it tapers lengthwise from 3 in. to 1 in. Make the taper cuts.

5 Rip-cut and cross-cut the remaining parts according to the dimensions in the cutting list, ganging up all parts with the same dimensions so you can cut them at the same setting on the table saw. Note that the front seat support and the center back support are bevel-ripped at 15° and 30°, respectively, on one edge. Make these cuts on a table saw. Use scrap wood of the same thickness and width to make test cuts, and adjust the rip fence to get the correct width of cut before ripping each part **(See Photo C).** Cut all eight back slats to full length.

6 Use a power sander to smooth out all contours, break the sharp edges, and smooth the wood sur-

PHOTO C: Bevel-rip one edge of the front seat support at 15°, using your table saw. The bevel should point away from the rip fence. Also bevel-rip the top edge of the center back support at a 30° angle.

PHOTO D: Attach the front seat support to the fronts of the rear legs using 2-in. galvanized deck screws driven into countersunk pilot holes. Cedar is soft wood, so take care not to drive the screws in too far.

faces (finish-sand the surfaces up to 150-grit).

ASSEMBLE THE SEAT
7 Attach the front seat support to the back legs so the ends of the seat support are flush with the outside surfaces of the legs. The beveled edge of the seat support should form a smooth, contiguous line with the contours of the top edges of the legs **(See Photo D).** Use 2-in. galvanized deck screws driven into countersunk pilot holes to attach the seat support. Glue isn't required, but use exterior glue if you choose to glue the joints.

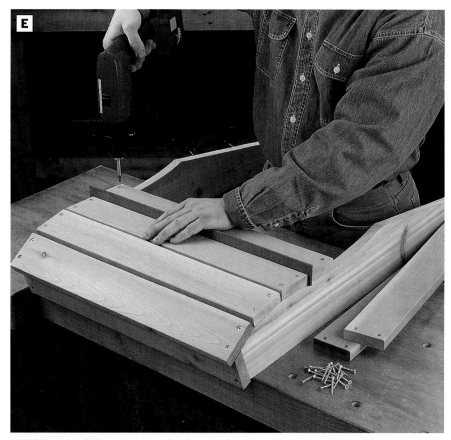

PHOTO E: Use a ¼-in. spacer to maintain equal distances between seat slats. Attach the slats by driving galvanized deck screws through countersunk pilot holes in the slats and into the top edges of the rear leg and the front seat support. Drive two screws at each joint. Because the screw heads will be visible, be careful to keep the screws aligned and spaced evenly.

PHOTO F: With the seat assembly braced so it's resting in position on a flat surface, position the front legs against the sides of the rear legs and mark reference lines on the front legs, following the bottom edges of each rear leg. Use the reference lines as a guide for attaching the front legs. The front legs should be set back 1 in. from the front edges of the rear legs.

❽ Starting at the front of the chair, screw the seat slats to the upper edges of the back legs using 1¼-in. galvanized deck screws. Position the front slat so it overhangs the front seat support by ½ in. Attach the second slat, leaving a slight gap (about ⅛ in.) between it and the front slat. Lay out the remaining slats so the space between slats is uniform (they should be about ¼ in.), then attach the remaining seat slats. Use a spacer to maintain consistent gaps (See Photo E).

❾ As an aid for attaching the front legs to the rear legs, cut a 10⁹⁄₁₆-in.-long spacer board from scrap to support the front edge of the rear leg/seat assembly. Clamp one leg in place 1 in. back from the front seat support and perfectly plumb. Draw reference lines on the inside of the front leg to mark the position of the top and bottom of the seat assembly (See Photo F). The whole setup can then be repositioned on its side to make it easier to screw from the inside. Drill countersunk pilot holes and drive four 1¼-in. galvanized deck screws at each joint. Attach both front legs.

❿ Use a combination square and pencil to mark a line down the outside of each front leg, 1-in. back from the front edge. Position the arm supports along this line, with their top edges flush with the tops of the legs. Attach the arm supports to the front legs with two 2-in. galvanized deck screws driven through countersunk pilot holes in the legs and into the inside edges of the arm supports. Make sure the screws are driven high enough up on the arm supports so they don't break through the outside edges of the supports (See Photo G).

MAKE THE BACK REST

⑪ The next step is to make the back rest assembly. First, screw the back slats to the front edge of the lower back support. The two outer slats should be set back ¼ in. from the ends of the support boards, and the bottoms of all slats should be flush with the bottom edges of the back support. For ease of assembly, clamp the lower back support along the front of your workbench, with the top edge flush with the benchtop. This will stabilize the setup and make it easier to position and screw the slats **(See Photo H)**. Use a ¼-in. spacer to give you a consistent gap between the slats. Drive a single 1¼-in. deck screw through the front of each slat and into the edge of the support board.

⑫ Turn the assembly over and screw the center and upper back supports to the back slats **(See Photo I)**. Position the upper back

PHOTO G: The arm supports are attached to the outer edges of the front legs to provide a surface for attaching and supporting the arms. Make sure to drive screws high enough on the arm supports that they don't penetrate the outer edge of the support.

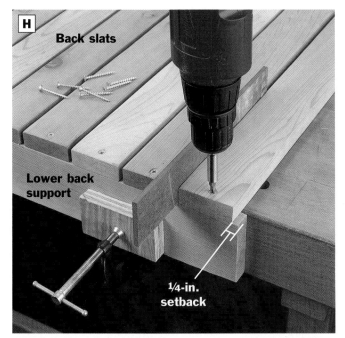

PHOTO H: Clamp the lower back support to your workbench so it's flush with the benchtop. Arrange the slats so the ends are flush with the support board edge, then attach them. Use a spacer to set the gap between slats. The outer slats should be set back ¼ in. from the ends of the support board.

PHOTO I: Attach the middle and upper back supports to the slats by driving 1 ¼-in. deck screws through the supports and into the back faces of the slats.

support 23¼ in. from the lower ends of the slats. The ends of the upper back support will be flush with the outer edges of the slats. Use the ¼-in. spacer to set the gaps. Position the center support 12 in. up from the lower ends of the slats. It should overhang the slats by 2⅝ in. at each end, and the beveled edge should face up, as shown in the drawings. Predrill and use one 1¼-in. countersunk deck screw per joint, driven through the supports and into the back faces of the slats.

⓭ The tops of the back slats are trimmed to form a semi-circle with a 12-in. radius. We used a strip of hardboard as a trammel for drawing the curved cutting line onto the slats. To make the trammel, cut a 13-in.-long strip of ¼-in.-thick hardboard and drill a ⅛-in.-dia. hole at one end and a 1⁄16-in.-dia. hole at the other end. The centerpoints of the holes should be 12 in. apart. Clamp a

PHOTO J: Scribe an arc with a 12-in. radius across the tops of the back slats to create a semicircular cutting line. We used a 13-in.-long strip of hardboard as a trammel for marking the cutting line.

PHOTO K: With the back rest assembly supported at the correct height by braces, begin attaching the back rest by driving screws through the lower support and into the tops of the rear legs.

PHOTO L: Use a counterbore/sink bit to drill countersunk pilot holes for the screws used to attach the arms. Drill at the location marks made on the arms using the template (See step 2). The holes should be countersunk just enough that the screw heads are recessed slightly.

scrap board across the back faces of the slats so the middle of the board is 12 in. down from the tops of the slats. At the gap between the two middle slats, measure down 12 in. from the tops of the slats and drive a wire nail through the smaller hole in the trammel and into the scrap board behind the gap between slats to anchor the trammel at the 12-in. mark. Insert a sharp pencil into the ⅛-in.-dia. hole at the other end of the trammel and draw the radius **(See Photo J).** Cut along the arched cutting line with a jig saw and smooth the edges.

ATTACH THE SEAT & BACK

⑭ Now the back assembly can be fixed to the seat assembly. Cut two 21-in. support braces from scrap wood. Put the back unit in place and clamp the supports against the back legs to position the center back support 21 in. off the floor **(See Photo K).** Align the fronts of the slats with the crest of the rear angle on the rear legs. Use two 2-in. screws to attach the lower back support to the back legs at each end. Leave the braces in place for now.

⑮ Drill countersunk pilot holes in the arms at the location marks made with the template **(See Photo L).** Use a scrap backing board and keep the drill plumb.

⑯ Place the arms in position. The back ends should overhang 1½ in. beyond the center back support. Attach the arms with four 2-in. deck screws in front and two 1¼-in. screws at the rear **(See Photo M).**

APPLY THE FINISH

⑰ Sand any remaining rough areas and wipe all surfaces with a tack cloth. Apply your finish of choice **(See Photo N).**

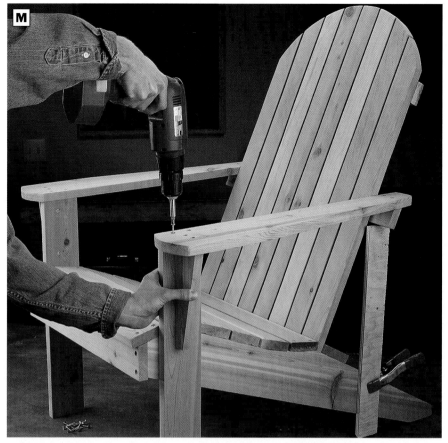

PHOTO M: Attach the arms by driving deck screws through counterbored pilot holes in the tops of the arms and down into the arm supports and center back support. Once the arms are attached, you can remove the support braces clamped to the back of the chair.

PHOTO N: Even exterior woods like cedar should be treated with wood preservative for protection and to prevent discoloration. A clear wood preservative with UV protection (shown above) will enhance wood tones and prevent graying from exposure.

CLEAR EXTERIOR FINISHES

Clear exterior finishes include clear wood preservative with UV protection (left) and exterior polyurethane (right) for a harder finish.

Workbench

Your workbench sets the tone for your workshop. From a discarded kitchen table or an old door laid across a pair of rickety sawhorses, to a gleaming oak masterpiece that looks too fancy to dine on, much less work on, there are just about as many styles of benches as there are woodworkers. The maple workbench built in this chapter is stylish enough for showing off, but it's designed to be used—and used hard. The design is simple enough that you can easily modify it to meet your special needs or tastes.

Vital Statistics: Workbench

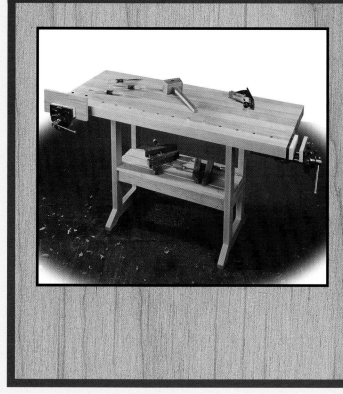

TYPE: Workbench

OVERALL SIZE: 60W by 36H by 24D

MATERIAL: Hard maple

JOINERY: Butt joints reinforced with lag screws, and dowel joints

CONSTRUCTION DETAILS:
· Solid maple, butcher-block style benchtop with 1,440 sq. in. of worksurface
· Storage shelf
· Adjustable bench dogs
· Comfortable 36-in. working height
· Permanent woodworking vises

FINISHING OPTIONS: Danish oil (one coat only) or other clear topcoat that can be refreshed easily, such as linseed oil.

Building time

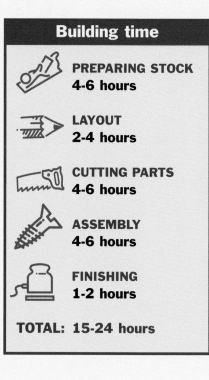

PREPARING STOCK
4-6 hours

LAYOUT
2-4 hours

CUTTING PARTS
4-6 hours

ASSEMBLY
4-6 hours

FINISHING
1-2 hours

TOTAL: 15-24 hours

Tools you'll use

· Surface planer
· Jointer
· Table saw
· Band saw or jig saw
· Circular saw
· Straightedge cutting guide
· Bar or pipe clamps
· Drill
· Belt sander or hand plane
· Combination square
· Doweling jig
· Drill guide
· Socket wrench and sockets

HANDYMAN Shopping list

- ☐ (4) 6/4 × 6 in. × 12 ft. hard maple boards
- ☐ (3) 6/4 × 4 in. × 8 ft. hard maple boards
- ☐ (2) 4/4 × 4 in. × 6 ft. hard maple boards
- ☐ (1 or 2) woodworker's bench vises
- ☐ (4-6) 3/4-in.-dia. brass bench dogs with square tops
- ☐ Wood glue
- ☐ #10 × 1½-in. wood screws
- ☐ 3/8 in. lag screws (1½ in., 2 in., 3 in.) with washers
- ☐ ½ × 2-in. fluted dowel pins
- ☐ Finishing materials

Workbench

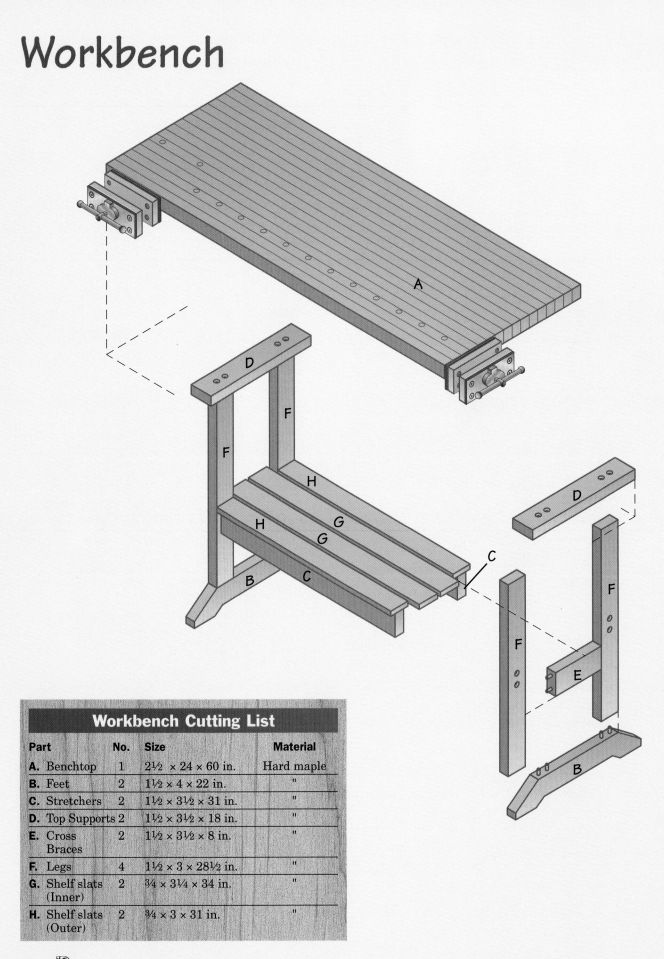

Workbench Cutting List

Part	No.	Size	Material
A. Benchtop	1	2½ × 24 × 60 in.	Hard maple
B. Feet	2	1½ × 4 × 22 in.	"
C. Stretchers	2	1½ × 3½ × 31 in.	"
D. Top Supports	2	1½ × 3½ × 18 in.	"
E. Cross Braces	2	1½ × 3½ × 8 in.	"
F. Legs	4	1½ × 3 × 28½ in.	"
G. Shelf slats (Inner)	2	¾ × 3¼ × 34 in.	"
H. Shelf slats (Outer)	2	¾ × 3 × 31 in.	"

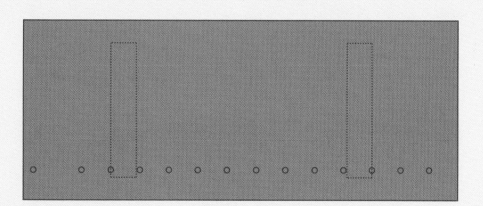

TOP VIEW

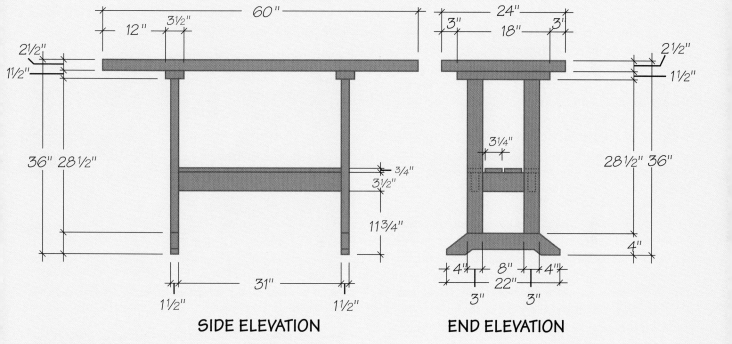

SIDE ELEVATION   **END ELEVATION**

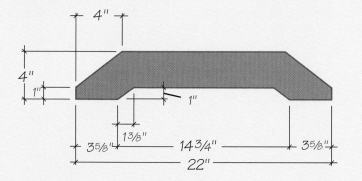

FOOT LAYOUT

MAKE THE LAMINATED BENCHTOP

Butcher-block style, face-laminated benchtops made from hardwood have several advantages: they are exceptionally stable from side to side and end to end; the worksurface itself consists of edge grain (or, in some cases, end grain), which is highly dent resistant and can be resurfaced easily after extended wear; and, because most hardwoods are very dense, the sheer weight of a solid hardwood benchtop results in a very sturdy worksurface. *Tip: The workbench project shown here has a 2½-in.-thick benchtop that was designed to accommodate a vise with 2½-in.-tall jaws. Because jaw size varies widely, it's a good idea to purchase your vise or vises before building the benchtop and modify the thickness of the top, if needed, to fit the particular vise you buy.*

1 Face-joint 6/4 hard maple stock to create smooth surfaces on both faces. This will result in boards not quite 1½ in. thick, but it's far more economical (and less time-consuming) than reducing 8/4 stock to 1½ in. thick. You can use a surface planer to smooth the boards, but it's important to joint the faces as well, since a planer will not square the stock. Prepare enough stock for 16, 62-in.-long × 2½-in.-wide boards.

2 Joint one edge of each board, then rip-cut them into 2½-in.-wide strips. Cross-cut the boards to 62 in. long (you'll trim off the excess length after the glue-up is completed). Lay out the wood strips side-by-side, 2½ in. high, on a flat worksurface. Clamp the strips together with a bar or pipe clamp, making sure the edges are all flush on the top surface of the benchtop. Draw reference lines 8 to 10 in. apart across the top, perpendicular to the joints, and number the boards in sequence.

3 Unclamp the boards and divide them into groups of four or five boards (for glue-ups involving more

PHOTO A: Face-glue the benchtop in sections of four or five boards, then face-glue the sections together.

PHOTO B: Flatten the top and bottom surfaces of the benchtop, using a belt sander or a hand plane.

PHOTO C: Drill holes for the bench dogs at approximately 6-in. intervals, using a portable drill guide to keep the holes straight.

PHOTO D: Use fluted, ½ × 2-in. dowel pins to reinforce the joints between the legs and the cross braces.

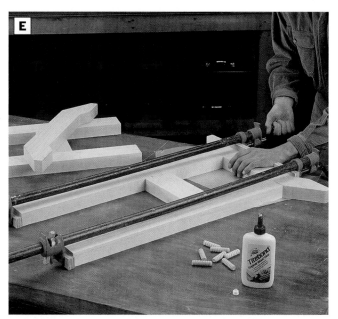

PHOTO E: Use pipe clamps to draw the feet tightly against the bottoms of the legs.

than four or five pieces of stock, it's easier to break up the project into smaller sections, then glue those sections together). Apply glue to the mating wood faces and glue up each section. Use bar or pipe clamps to draw the boards together, and keep the edges of the boards flush (the ends can stagger slightly, since they'll be trimmed square later).

❹ After the glue on the benchtop sections has cured, glue the sections together to create the benchtop **(See Photo A).** Take care to keep the edges flush at the top and bottom of the benchtop—wood cauls clamped above and below the benchtop are helpful for this purpose. Alternate bar or pipe clamps above and below the glue-up to equalize clamping pressure. Only tighten the clamps until the joints are tight; don't overtighten or you can squeeze the joints dry of glue. Leave the clamps on until the glue cures.

❺ Scrape the dried glue from both sides, and level the top and bottom surfaces using a belt sander or hand plane. If using a belt sander, avoid sanding belts coarser than 100-grit, and make initial sanding passes diagonally across the glue joints **(See Photo B).** If using a hand plane, plane diagonally across the grain until the surface is flat, then plane with the grain. Finish smoothing with a cabinet scraper or sandpaper. Run a long straightedge over the surfaces to test for flatness. A perfectly flat worksurface is very important to successful woodworking, so it's worth investing some time and energy into achieving a perfectly flat top.

❻ Use a circular saw with a straightedge cutting guide fence to trim the ends of the benchtop so it's 60 in. long. Trim some stock from both ends, making sure the ends are square to the edges of the top.

❼ Mark a layout line for drilling guide holes for the bench dogs. We used a ¾-in.-dia. brad-point bit to drill the guide holes for the ¾-in.-dia. dogs we purchased. If the vise you'll be installing on the end of your bench has a pop-up bench dog, draw the layout line so it's aligned with the center of the vise dog after the vise is installed. Otherwise, center the line with the midpoint of the vise jaw. We drilled guide holes every 6 in. Use a portable drill guide to ensure that the holes are exactly vertical **(See Photo C).**

BUILD THE BASE

❽ Rip four 1½-in.-thick boards to 3 in. wide, then cross-cut them to 28½ in. to make the legs. Rip the two 1½-in.-thick leg cross braces to 3½ in. wide, then cut them to a length of 8 in.

❾ Draw square lines across the inside edges of the legs for the placement of the cross braces. The lower lines should be 7¾ in. up from the bottoms of the legs, and the upper lines should be 3½ in. above the lower lines. Lay out holes for two ½ × 2-in. fluted dowels per joint and drill holes with a dowel drilling guide. Glue the dowels and joints and clamp up two legs to a cross support, padding the clamps to protect the wood **(See Photo D).** Check the squareness by measuring to make sure the distance between the

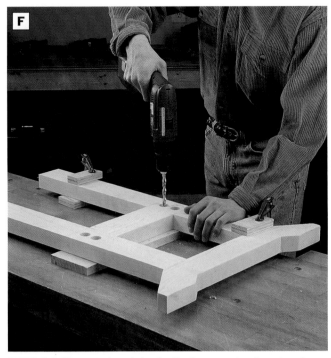

PHOTO F: Drill counterbore holes for the lag screw heads and washers, and drill clearance holes and pilot holes for the shanks of the screws.

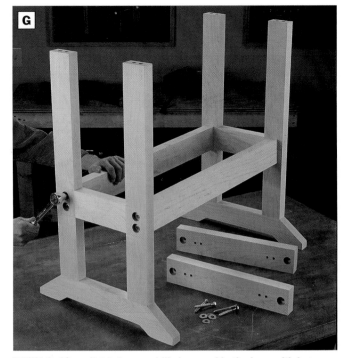

PHOTO G: After pilot holes are drilled, assemble the base with lag screws and washers driven with a socket wrench.

tops of the legs and the bottoms is the same. Make both side assemblies.

⑩ Cut the feet to 4 × 22 in. Lay out the angled cutting lines by marking out the measurements shown in the *Foot layout drawing* on page 31. Use a straightedge to draw lines connecting these marks. Cut out the shape of the feet with a band saw or jig saw. Sand the sawn edges smooth.

⑪ Lay out and drill dowel holes connecting the ends of the legs to the tops of the feet. Glue and clamp the feet to the legs **(See Photo E).**

⑫ Rip the two leg stretchers and the two leg top supports to 3½ in. wide from 1½ in. stock. Cross-cut the stretchers to 31 in. and the supports to 18 in.

⑬ Continue the cross support layout lines already on the legs, squaring them across the faces of the legs to serve as placement lines for the leg stretchers. Mark lines for the thickness of the stretchers, centered on the legs. Mark centerpoints for two lag-screw pilot holes at each joint. Drill ¾-in.-dia. × ⅜-in.-deep counterbores for each hole, then drill ¼-in. pilots through the center of each counterbored hole **(See Photo F).**

⑭ Position the stretchers between the side assemblies and assemble the base temporarily by clamping across the leg cross supports. Line the stretchers up with their marks and drill pilot holes through the lag holes into the ends of the stretchers. Drill counterbored holes in the top supports, then center the top supports on the legs and drill pilot holes into the tops of the legs. Also drill guide holes for the lag screws that attach the top supports to the underside of the benchtop.

⑮ Attach the legs to the ends of the leg stretchers with ⅜ × 3-in. lag screws fitted with ⅜-in. washers **(See Photo G).** Bolt the leg top supports to the tops of the legs with the same size lag screws.

INSTALL THE SHELF

⑯ Plane ¼ maple down to ¾ in. thick to make the shelf slats. Rip-cut and cross-cut the inner and outer slats to size.

⑰ Lay the outside shelf slats onto the stretchers, with their edges flush with the sides of the legs. Drill a countersunk pilot hole for a #10 × 1½-in. flathead wood screw near each end of each outer slat, centered over the stretcher below.

⑱ Place the inside shelf slats on the leg cross braces with their ends flush with the braces. Use ½-in.

PHOTO H: Screw the inner and outer slats to the stretchers and cross braces to create a storage shelf.

PHOTO I: Center the base on the underside of the benchtop, then attach it with lag screws driven through the top supports.

spacer blocks between slats to ensure even gaps. Drill a pair of countersunk pilot holes at the end of each inner slat, centered over the cross brace below. Drive two #10 × 1½-in. flathead wood screws at each end **(See Photo H)**.

ATTACH THE BENCHTOP

19 Sand all parts to 150-grit and ease all sharp edges.

20 Lay the benchtop upside-down and center the base on the underside of the top. Drill counterbored pilot holes into the top and attach the leg top supports to the underside of the top with washers and ⅜ × 3-in. lag screws **(See Photo I)**.

APPLY FINISHING TOUCHES

21 Read the manufacturer's instructions for installing your bench vises. Cut hardwood jaw plates and screw them to the metal jaws through the jaw holes on the vise. Make up the appropriate filler blocks to shim each vise so the top edges of the jaws are flush with the benchtop. The vises we selected for our bench are installed with ⅜ × 2-in. lag screws driven up through the underside of the vise and into the benchtop **(See Photo J)**.

22 Apply a protective finish to the workbench. We used a single coat of Danish oil. Do not apply more

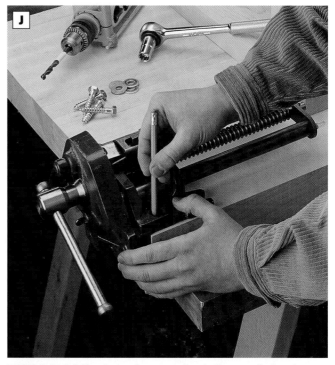

PHOTO J: Install the vise or vises according to the manufacturer's installation instructions (they may differ from model to model).

than one coat of finishing material, since multiple layers make the surface more slippery. Every other year or so, depending on wear, remove the oil finish with mineral spirits, sand the surface, and apply a fresh finish.

Oak Cabinets

Store your best table linens and display your favorite china, glassware or curios in this handsome, efficient pair of stacked oak cabinets. Constructed as two separate units, the upper and lower cabinets are attached together to form a hutch-style storage unit that's at home in a dining room, kitchen or even a living room.

Vital Statistics: Oak Cabinets

TYPE: Storage and display cabinet

OVERALL SIZE: 36W by 75H by 16D

MATERIAL: Red oak, oak plywood and glass

JOINERY: Rabbet joints, double-rabbet joints, dowel joints

CONSTRUCTION DETAILS:

· Upper cabinet fitted with glass doors in oak frame
· Lower cabinet has two 8 × 14 × 31-in. drawers
· Oak trim is profiled with ogee router bit
· Sturdy base structure
· Decorative crown molding frame on upper cabinet
· Visible carcase panels made from solid oak

FINISHING OPTIONS: Stain with clear topcoat

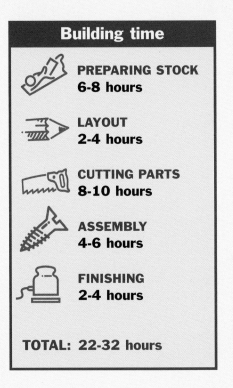

Building time

PREPARING STOCK
6-8 hours

LAYOUT
2-4 hours

CUTTING PARTS
8-10 hours

ASSEMBLY
4-6 hours

FINISHING
2-4 hours

TOTAL: 22-32 hours

Tools you'll use

· Table saw
· Jointer
· Power miter saw
· Jig saw or hand saw
· Router and router table with straight, rabbet and ogee bits
· Drill/driver
· Tape measure and metal rule
· Combination square
· 36-in. or longer bar or pipe clamps (8)
· C-clamps
· Hammer or tack hammer
· Screwdriver
· Wood chisels
· Doweling jig
· Nailset
· Pegboard drilling guide

Shopping list

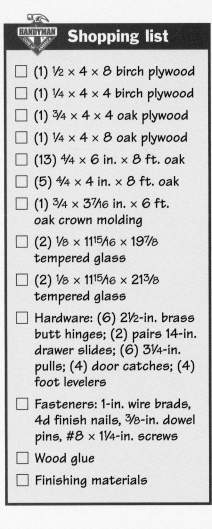

- [ ] (1) ½ × 4 × 8 birch plywood
- [ ] (1) ¼ × 4 × 4 birch plywood
- [ ] (1) ¾ × 4 × 4 oak plywood
- [ ] (1) ¼ × 4 × 8 oak plywood
- [ ] (13) 4/4 × 6 in. × 8 ft. oak
- [ ] (5) 4/4 × 4 in. × 8 ft. oak
- [ ] (1) ¾ × 3⁷⁄₁₆ in. × 6 ft. oak crown molding
- [ ] (2) ⅛ × 11¹⁵⁄₁₆ × 19⁷⁄₈ tempered glass
- [ ] (2) ⅛ × 11¹⁵⁄₁₆ × 21³⁄₈ tempered glass
- [ ] Hardware: (6) 2½-in. brass butt hinges; (2) pairs 14-in. drawer slides; (6) 3¼-in. pulls; (4) door catches; (4) foot levelers
- [ ] Fasteners: 1-in. wire brads, 4d finish nails, ⅜-in. dowel pins, #8 × 1¼-in. screws
- [ ] Wood glue
- [ ] Finishing materials

Base Cutting List

Part		No.	Size	Material
A.	Foot Blocks	4	$1\frac{1}{2} \times 1\frac{1}{2} \times 4\frac{1}{4}$ in.	Poplar
B.	Bottom	1	$\frac{1}{2} \times 15\frac{1}{4} \times 34\frac{1}{2}$ in.	Birch plywood
C.	Base side	2	$\frac{3}{4} \times 5\frac{1}{2} \times 16$ in.	Red oak
D.	Base front	1	$\frac{3}{4} \times 5\frac{1}{2} \times 36$ in.	"

Lower Cabinet Cutting List

Part		No.	Size	Material
E.	Sides	2	$\frac{3}{4} \times 15\frac{1}{4} \times 18\frac{3}{8}$ in.	Red oak
F.	Top	1	$\frac{3}{4} \times 15\frac{1}{4} \times 34\frac{1}{2}$ in.	"
G.	Bottom	1	$\frac{3}{4} \times 15\frac{1}{4} \times 34\frac{1}{2}$ in.	Oak plywood
H.	Back panel	1	$\frac{1}{4} \times 33\frac{5}{8} \times 18\frac{1}{4}$ in.	"
I.	Trim	3	$\frac{3}{4} \times \frac{3}{4} \times$ Cut to fit	Red oak

Upper Cabinet Cutting List

Part		No.	Size	Material
J.	Sides	2	$\frac{3}{4} \times 10\frac{3}{4} \times 49$ in.	Red oak
K.	Top/bottom	2	$\frac{3}{4} \times 11\frac{9}{16} \times 32$ in.	"
L.	Adj. shelves	2	$\frac{3}{4} \times 9\frac{11}{16} \times 30\frac{1}{4}$ in.	Oak plywood
M.	Back panel	1	$\frac{1}{4} \times 31\frac{1}{8} \times 48\frac{1}{8}$ in.	"
N.	Stiles	4	$\frac{3}{4} \times 2\frac{1}{4} \times 47\frac{3}{8}$ in.	Red oak
O.	Rails (top)	2	$\frac{3}{4} \times 2\frac{1}{8} \times 11\frac{7}{16}$ in.	"
P.	Rails (mid)	2	$\frac{3}{4} \times 2\frac{1}{4} \times 11\frac{7}{16}$ in.	"
Q.	Rails (btm)	2	$\frac{3}{4} \times 2\frac{3}{4} \times 11\frac{7}{16}$ in.	"
R.	Retainer	8	$\frac{1}{4} \times \frac{3}{8} \times$ Cut to fit	"
S.	Light (upper)	2	$\frac{1}{8} \times 11\frac{15}{16} \times 19\frac{7}{8}$ in.	Glass
T.	Light (lower)	2	$\frac{1}{8} \times 11\frac{15}{16} \times 21\frac{3}{8}$ in.	"
U.	Crown	3	$\frac{3}{4} \times 3\frac{7}{16} \times$ Cut to fit	Red oak
V.	Trim	5	$\frac{3}{4} \times \frac{3}{4} \times$ Cut to fit	"

Drawer Cutting List

Part		No.	Size	Material
W.	Sides	4	$\frac{1}{2} \times 8 \times 14$ in.	Plywood
X.	Front/back	4	$\frac{1}{2} \times 8 \times 31\frac{1}{2}$ in.	"
Y.	Bottom	2	$\frac{1}{4} \times 13\frac{1}{2} \times 31\frac{1}{2}$ in.	"
Z.	Drawer front	2	$\frac{3}{4} \times 8\frac{3}{4} \times 34\frac{1}{2}$ in.	Red oak

Oak Cabinets

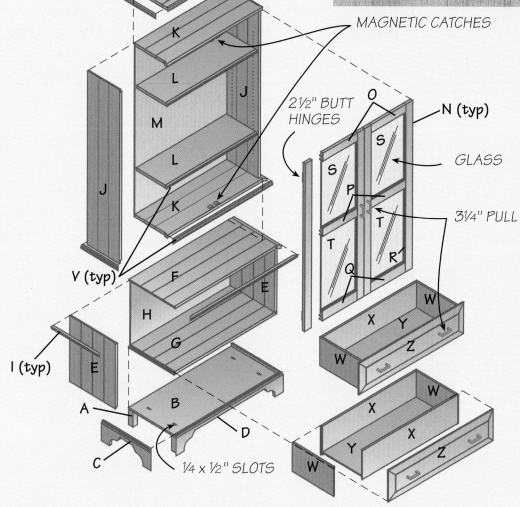

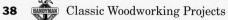

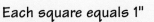
Each square equals 1"

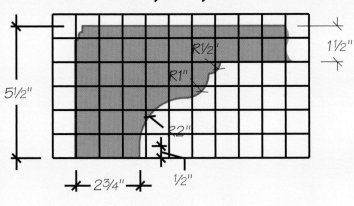

BASE PATTERN

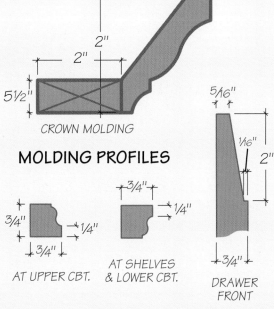

CROWN MOLDING

MOLDING PROFILES

AT UPPER CBT.

AT SHELVES & LOWER CBT.

DRAWER FRONT

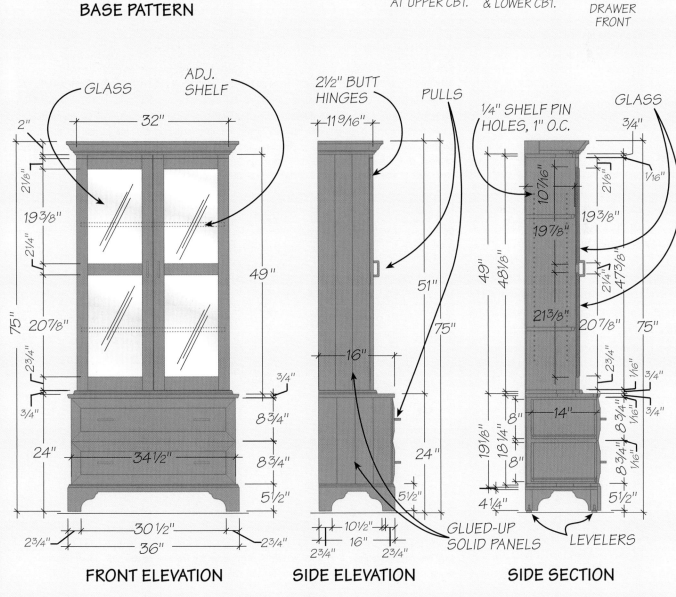

GLASS

ADJ. SHELF

2½" BUTT HINGES

PULLS

¼" SHELF PIN HOLES, 1" O.C.

GLASS

GLUED-UP SOLID PANELS

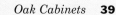

LEVELERS

FRONT ELEVATION

SIDE ELEVATION

SIDE SECTION

BUILD THE CABINET CARCASES
The upper and lower cabinets in this project are built using the same basic principles and techniques used to make kitchen cabinets and other forms of casework. Except for the back panels and the bottom panel of the lower cabinet (which is hidden by drawers and thus made of plywood), all the panels used to make the carcases are made from glued-up strips of red oak.

❶ Create edge-glued panels for the sides, top and bottom of the upper cabinet, and the sides and top of the lower cabinet. We used 4/4 × 4-in. red oak to make the panels. Plane the individual boards down to slightly more than 3/4 in. thick before jointing, ripping to width and square, and gluing them up. NOTE: *If you have a surface planer with more than a 15-in. width capacity, you can plane down all the panels after the glue-up.* We used biscuits for alignment and to reinforce the glue joints. If you're gluing up long panels and then cross-cutting the individual parts to length, plan the biscuit layout so the biscuits don't cross the cutting lines.

❷ Rip-cut, cross-cut and plane the panels to finished size for the carcase parts. Also cut a bottom panel for the lower cabinet from

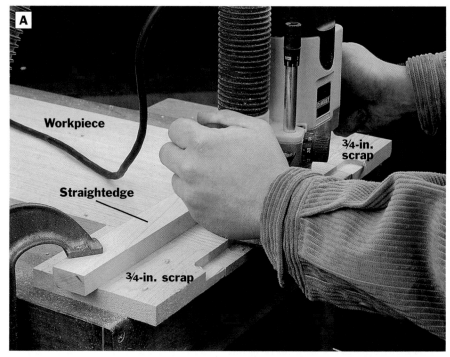

PHOTO A: Cut 3/4 × 3/8-in.-deep rabbets in the top and bottom of the side panels for the upper cabinet, and cut 3/8 × 3/8-in.-deep rabbets in the top and bottom of the side panels for the lower cabinet. Also cut 3/8 × 3/8-in.-deep rabbets in the ends of the top and bottom panels for the lower cabinet. Use a router and straight bit to make the cuts. Clamp pieces of 3/4-in.-thick scrap on each side of the workpiece, and clamp a straightedge cutting guide for the router to follow.

Workpiece
Straightedge
3/4-in. scrap
3/4-in. scrap

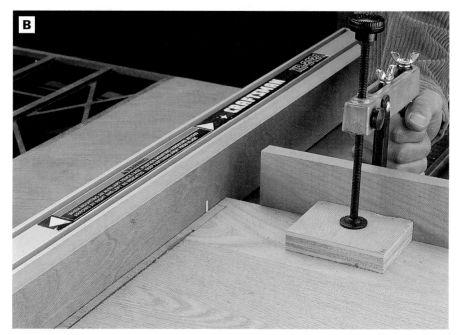

PHOTO B: Cut notches in the ends of the upper cabinet's top and bottom panels. Stop the cuts before the blade cuts past the end line of the cuts, and finish the cuts with a hand saw or jig saw. The notches create a 3/8 × 3/4-in. tab that fits over the front edge the side panel on the upper cabinet, creating a recess below for the cabinet door frames.

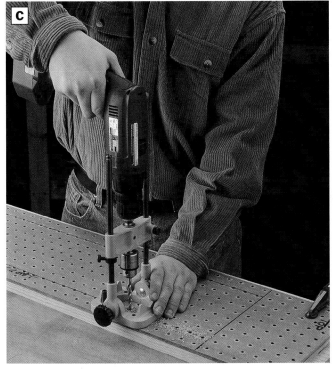

PHOTO C: Drill shelf pin holes in the sides of the upper cabinet, using pegboard as a template. Orient the guide the same way on facing sides to ensure that the holes are aligned.

PHOTO D: Cut ¼ × ¼-in. rabbets into the back edges of the side, top and bottom panels to create recesses for the back panels. We used a router with a piloted rabbet bit.

PILOTED RABBET BITS

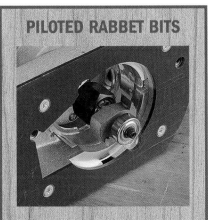

Piloted router bits have a bearing or a fixed spindle that follows the edge of a board as you cut, allowing the cutters to engage the wood and maintain a uniform depth of cut without the need for a straightedge guide. Piloted rabbet bits, like the one shown above, are generally available in sizes that will cut rabbets ranging from ¼ in. to ¾ in. deep.

¾-in. plywood. Cut ¾-in. × ⅜-in.-deep rabbets in the top and bottom edges of the side panels for the upper cabinet. Cut ⅜-in. × ⅜-in.-deep rabbets in the top and bottom edges of the side panels for the lower cabinet, as well as in the ends of the top and bottom panels. The carcase joints in the lower cabinet are double-rabbet joints, and the upper carcase uses single-rabbet joints. We used a router with a ¾-in. straight bit to cut the rabbets **(See Photo A).**

❸ The top and bottom panels in the upper cabinet extend past the front edges of the side panels by ¾ in. to create a recess for the flush-mounted cabinet doors (which are attached with hinges to the front edges of the side panels). The front edges of the top and bottom panels should overlay the edges of the side panels. For this reason, cut a ⅜-in.-wide notch that starts at the back of

the top and bottom panel, on each end, and stops ¾ in. from each front edge. Draw an outline of the waste material being removed at each end of the top and bottom panels, then set up your table saw and cut most of the way from the back to the front. Stop the cut short of the end line and finish it with a hand saw or jig saw. Cut into the end of each panel to remove the waste, leaving a ⅜-in.-wide tab at each front end **(See Photo B).**

❹ Drill two rows of holes for adjustable shelf pins in each side of the upper carcase. We used a piece of perforated hardboard (pegboard) for a drilling template **(See Photo C).** Our plan called for shelf pins made from ¼-in. doweling, so we drilled ¼-in.-dia. × ⅜-in.-deep holes. We spaced the holes 1 in. apart on-center to allow for maximum adjustability. But if you do a little planning up

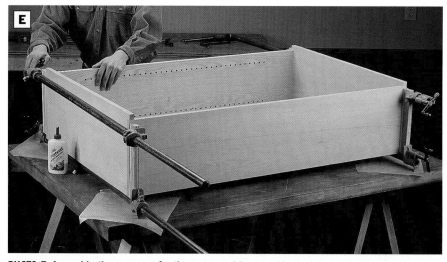

PHOTO E: Assemble the carcases for the upper and lower cabinets. Use pairs of bar or pipe clamps and wood cauls to draw the panels together. Positioning the back panel in the back panel recess serves as a helpful reference for squaring the carcase.

PHOTO F: Attach the foot blocks to the corners of the plywood base with glue and screws. Note the screw slots cut into the platform for attaching the base to the lower cabinet carcase.

PHOTO G: Cut the pattern shapes in the base trim pieces. We used a jig saw. Wait until you've cut the miters before making the contour cuts so you can be sure each cutout shape is centered and the correct distance from the ends of the trim piece.

front, you can eliminate most of the holes (and their "knock-down" look) by planning your shelf height and drilling only one or two holes for each shelf pin. Use a portable drill guide with a depth stop to ensure the holes are perpendicular and the same depth.

5 Cut ¼ × ¼-in. rabbets in the back edges of the sides, top and bottom of each cabinet. This will create ¼-in.-deep recesses for the back panels when the carcases are assembled. Use a router with a ¼-in.-dia. piloted rabbet bit to make the cuts **(See Photo D)**. Since the rabbets can run the full lengths of the parts, a table saw with a dado-blade set also could be used.

6 Cut the back panel to size for each cabinet from ¼-in. plywood.

7 Finish-sand the carcase parts. Glue and clamp together the carcases for the upper **(See Photo E)** and lower cabinets. Set the back panel in the recess at the back of each cabinet (without glue) to help square them up. Also check for squareness by measuring across the diagonals. Adjust the clamps as necessary. Use wood cauls to distribute the clamping pressure evenly. After the glue has cured, remove the clamps, then tack the back panels into the recesses with 1-in. wire nails.

BUILD THE BASE STRUCTURE
Unlike kitchen cabinets that are attached permanently, movable cupboards, cabinets and hutches require some type of sturdy base structure for support. For our oak cabinets, we decided to build a simple plywood platform supported by four square legs. The structure is trimmed with profiled red oak. And because wood movement is an issue with solid-wood cabi-

PHOTO H: The trim pieces wrap around the base structure, adding decoration and "feet" to the cabinets. Use 4d finish nails and glue to attach the mitered trim pieces. Drill pilot holes for the nails (you can remove the head from a finish nail and chuck it into your drill if you don't have a drill bit small enough for the job). Set nails with a nailset.

PHOTO I: Attach the base to the underside of the lower cabinet with screws and washers. The screw slots in the platform allow the screws to move as the wood moves.

nets like those shown here, we cut screw slots in the platform so the screws used to attach the lower cabinet to the base structure can move with the wood.

8 Cut a piece of ½-in. construction-grade plywood the same dimensions as the plywood bottom panel for the lower cabinet (if all you have on hand is ¾-in. plywood, you may use that instead, but be sure to subtract ¼-in. from the height of the foot blocks that attach to the platform). Cut four ¼-in.-wide × 1-in.-long screw slots, running front-to-back, about 4 in. in from each corner of the bottom platform board.

9 Cut four hardwood foot blocks, 1½-in.-square × 4½-in.-long. Apply glue, then drive a countersunk wood screw through the platform and down into each foot block **(See Photo F).**

10 The trim boards for the base feature an ogee profile, cut with a router, along the top edges and decorative cutouts on the bottom to create "feet" for the base. They are mitered together at the front corners. To make the trim pieces, rip-cut to 5½ in. wide a ¾-in.-thick strip of red oak that's at least 72 in. long.

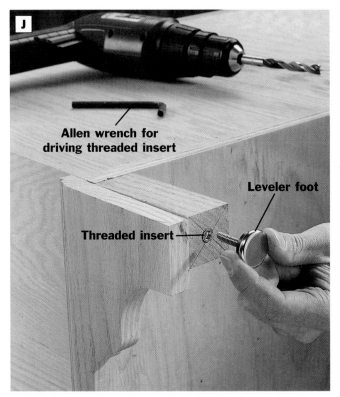

PHOTO J: Leveler feet are attached to the foot blocks to protect the floor and to allow you to adjust the height of the cabinet to conform to unevenness in the floor.

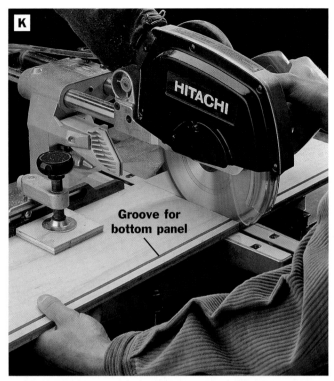

PHOTO K: The sides, front and back for each drawer can be cut from a single 8-ft.-long strip of ½-in. plywood. By cutting the groove for the drawer bottom before cross-cutting the parts, you can ensure that the groove will line up on all four parts.

PHOTO L: The glued double-rabbet joints used to construct the drawer boxes are strong enough that no additional reinforcement is needed. Do not use glue or fasteners to secure the drawer bottom, which is inserted into the inside grooves prior to drawer assembly.

⓫ On a router table, rout an ogee profile along the top edge of the workpiece, using a ¾-in. ogee bit.

⓬ Cut the three base trim pieces to length, mitering the ends to form the front joints and making square cuts on the back ends of the side pieces. Make the mitered cuts on a table saw, using a miter gauge, or with a miter box (hand or power).

⓭ Enlarge the *Base pattern* from page 39 to size and transfer it to the front of each trim piece, starting 2¾ in. from each end (reverse the pattern for the right side of each cutout). Cut out the shapes along the waste sides of the lines with a jig saw or scroll saw (**See Photo G**). Sand or file the edges smooth.

⓮ Attach the trim to the base. Apply glue to the front and side edges of the plywood, the outside faces of the foot blocks, and the mitered corners of the trim. Use 4d finish nails to fasten the trim to the foot blocks and the edges of the plywood. Set the nails below the surface of the wood with a nailset (**See Photo H**). Make sure the bottom edges of the trim are flush with the bottoms of the foot blocks (the tops of the trim pieces should extend ¾ in. past the top of the plywood platform).

ATTACH THE LOWER CABINET TO THE BASE

⓯ Turn the lower cabinet carcase upside-down and screw the base structure to the carcase bottom through the centers of the slotted holes, using #8 × 1¼-in. wood screws with washers (**See Photo I**). Drill pilot holes into the bottom of the lower cabinet.

⓰ Install foot leveler hardware into the bottom of each foot block. First, find the centerpoints in the bottoms of the foot blocks by using a miter square or a straightedge to draw diagonal lines connecting the corners. Drill guide holes for the threaded inserts, according to the manufacturer's specifications. Then insert the threaded inserts and thread the leveler feet into the inserts (**See Photo J**).

MAKE & HANG THE DRAWERS
The lower cabinet is fitted with two large drawers for convenient storage. If it better meets your needs, you could replace the drawers with shelves and cabinet doors, as in the upper cabinet. To save on materials cost, we made the drawers out of plywood, then attached a solid-oak drawer front to each drawer.

⓱ Rip-cut two 8-in.-wide strips from an 8-ft.-long sheet of ½-in.

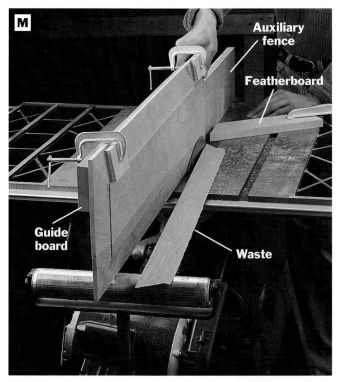

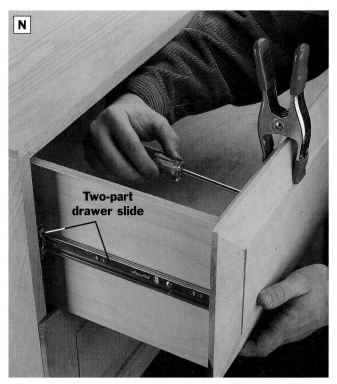

PHOTO M: Make 10° bevel cuts on all four sides of each drawer front face to create raised panels. Install a tall auxiliary fence and clamp a guide board onto the back of the panel high enough so it will ride on top of the auxiliary fence as you feed the workpiece into the blade.

PHOTO N: Attach the drawer fronts to the drawers with screws driven through the front, inside face of the drawer box and into the back face of the raised-panel drawer front. Hang the drawer boxes first so the drawer fronts will be perfectly positioned.

plywood to make the drawer sides, front and back (one strip is enough material to make all four parts for each drawer). Cut a ¼ × ¼-in. dado in one face of each strip, ½ in. up from the bottom edge. This will be the groove to hold the drawer bottom. The dado can be cut on a table saw or a router table.

⓲ Cross-cut the drawer sides, fronts and backs to length (See Photo K).

⓳ On the ends of each of the drawer sides, cut ¼ × ¼-in. rabbets on the inside faces for double-rabbet joints.

⓴ Cut the drawer bottoms to size from ¼-in. plywood or hardboard.

㉑ Glue and clamp the drawer boxes together, with the bottoms captured in (but not glued into)

their grooves (See Photo L).

㉒ Hang the drawer boxes inside the lower cabinet. Use two full-extension, 14-in. metal drawer slides for each drawer. Follow the hardware manufacturer's instructions for positioning the slides, and be sure to allow for the 8¾ × 34½-in. drawer fronts that will be attached to the drawer boxes.

㉓ Cut the drawer faces to size. You'll need to glue up two strips of oak if you don't have any stock that's wider than 8 in.

㉔ Cut a raised panel bevel into each drawer front on the table saw. Tilt the saw blade to 10°, and set the cutting height to 2 in. Set the rip fence 5⁄16 in. away from the blade (the tilt of the blade should be facing away from the rip fence). Make a bevel cut along all four edges of each drawer front. Using

a featherboard and a tall auxiliary fence, make a test cut into ¾-in. scrap: The top of the bevel cut should form a square ledge about ¹⁄16 in. wide (roughly the thickness of the saw blade), as shown in the *Drawer front* diagram on page 39. Adjust the blade tilt or cutting height as needed until the profile of the cut is correct. Cut all four edges of each drawer front to create a raised center panel (See Photo M).

㉕ Attach the drawer fronts to the drawer boxes. First, hang the drawer boxes in the lower cabinet. Then, position the drawer fronts against the drawers and adjust them until they are centered on the drawer openings and there is a gap of about ¹⁄16 to ⅛ in. between the drawer fronts. Clamp the drawer fronts to the drawer boxes. Attach the drawer fronts by driving four #6 × 1-in. round-head

PHOTO O: After the molding profile has been routed into the edge of a wide, ¾-in.-thick oak board, rip-cut a ¾-in.-wide strip of the molding on the table saw. Repeat the process to make up as much molding as you'll need (about 13 lineal feet for the project as shown). This process is easier and safer than ripping the molding to width first and trying to feed narrow strips across a large cutter on the router table.

PHOTO P: Make dowel joints at all the rail/stile joints on each cabinet door, then glue the joints and assemble the door frames. Position a bar or pipe clamp beneath each rail location and use clamp pads to protect the wood.

Classic Woodworking Projects

screws, with washers, through the inside faces of the drawer boxes and into the backs of the drawer fronts (See Photo N).

ATTACH THE CABINET TRIM

The bottom of the upper cabinet, the top of the lower cabinet and the front edges of the upper cabinet shelves are trimmed with ¾ × ¾-in. molding strips. We cut our own trim using a ¾-in. ogee bit, but you could purchase premilled molding with a similar profile if you don't have a router table.

㉖ Plane oak stock to a thickness of ¾ in. and square one edge on your jointer. Prepare enough stock to cut eight trim pieces of the following lengths: (2) 12 in.; (2) 18 in.; (4) 34 in.

㉗ Mount a ¾-in. ogee bit into your router table and cut an ogee profile along the jointed edge of each piece of oak stock. On your table saw, rip-cut a ¾-in.-wide strip from the profiled edges of the stock (See Photo O). Repeat this to make up as much trim as you need.

㉘ Miter-cut the molding to length to fit around the bottom edge of the upper cabinet and the top edge of the lower cabinet. Note that the molding on the upper cabinet is installed with the profile facing up, but on the lower cabinet and the upper cabinet shelves the profile faces down. Cut the adjustable shelves to size (if you haven't already). Attach the molding with glue and 1¼-in. wire nails. *NOTE: To allow for wood movement, attach molding to the short sides of the top of the bottom cabinet with nails only—no glue.* Set the nailheads. Make sure the trim pieces are flush with the the top surface of the cabinet part to which they're being attached.

Make the
Upper Cabinet Doors

We built glass doors for the upper cabinet to allow the cabinet to be used for display purposes. The doors consist of oak face frames and ⅛-in. tempered glass panels.

㉙ Cut the door rails and stiles to size from ¾-in.-thick oak.

㉚ The rails are joined to the stiles with butt joints reinforced by dowels. Arrange the rails and stiles for each door and mark the locations of the rails onto the stiles according to the *Front elevation* drawing on page 39. Lay out and drill holes for dowel joints, using a doweling jig.

㉛ Assemble the door frames with glue and clamps **(See Photo P).** Check the diagonal measurements and adjust the clamps as needed to bring the frames into square.

㉜ Rabbet the inside back edges of the door frames to accept the glass panels **(See Photo Q).** Use a ¼-in. piloted rabbet bit to cut ¼-in.-wide × ½-in.-deep rabbets all around both openings in each door. Scribe the corners of the rabbet recesses with a straightedge and utility knife, and chisel out the corners until they're square.

㉝ Lay out and cut mortises for 2½-in. butt hinges on each door. We used three brass butt hinges per door. The hinges are spaced 2 in. up from the bottom and 2 in. down from the top. The middle hinge is centered between the top and bottom hinges. Trace around a hinge leaf on the door stiles to make cutting lines for the mortises. Before chiseling out the mortises, score along the edge of the

PHOTO Q: Rout a ¼ × ⅜-in.-deep rabbet recess around the perimeter of each opening in the upper cabinet doors. Use a ¼-in. piloted rabbet bit (See page 41) to make the cuts. Square off the rounded corners left by the router bit, using a sharp chisel. To keep the wood from tearing, score along the chisel lines with a sharp knife before squaring the corners.

PHOTO R: Chisel mortises for the hinges into the inside faces of the outer door stiles and into the front edges of the cabinet sides. Use one of the leaves from the 2½-in. butt hinges as a template for tracing the cutting lines for the mortises.

PHOTO S: Miter-cut the ends of the front crown molding strip and the front end of each side strip at 45° to make the crown molding assembly that is attached to the top of the upper cabinet. We used a simple crown molding miter jig to set up the cuts on our power miter saw.

PHOTO T: Attach the crown frame to the top of the cabinet with screws and washers. The screw slots in the tops of the scrap wood backer frame allow for cross-grain expansion and contraction of the solid wood top.

cutting lines to keep the wood from splintering. Use a sharp wood chisel (the same width as the mortise, if possible) to cut out each mortise to a depth equal to the thickness of the hinge leaf **(See Photo R).**

34 Position each cabinet door in the door opening, making sure the outside edge of each door is flush with the edge of the cabinet. Mark the locations of the hinge mortises on the cabinet, then remove the doors. Lay out and cut hinge mortises at the correct locations in the front edge of each cabinet side. Do not hang the cabinet doors yet.

ATTACH THE CROWN MOLDING

We framed the top of the upper cabinet with crown molding for a nice decorative touch. Although it's possible to make crown molding yourself, using a shaper or molding cutters in the table saw, we purchased premilled, 3⁷⁄16-in. red oak crown molding. If you've never tried to make miter joints with crown molding before, you may want to pick up some inexpensive pine or mahogany molding to practice your cutting skills before you cut into the oak stock. To simplify the process, we built a frame the same dimensions as the top of the cabinet, using scrap wood (we used 1 × 2-in. pine). Then, we attached the crown molding to the frame and mounted the assembly to the top of the cabinet. The main advantage to this method is that you can build the scrap frame so the corners are precisely square (no matter how careful you've been with the cabinet assembly, it's likely that the carcase is slightly out of square by this point, which will throw off the miter angles for the crown molding).

35 Mitered joints on crown molding require tricky compound angles. We built a simple jig for our power miter saw and used it to accurately cut the corners of the molding **(See Photo S).** To build the jig, cut a wide board (10 in. or so) and a narrow board (2 in. or so) to about 1 ft. in length, and butt-join them together into an "L" shape. Be very careful that the narrow board (the fence of the jig) is perpendicular to the wider board. Set a piece of the crown molding into the jig so one of the flared edges on the back side of the molding is flush against the fence of the jig, and the other flared edge is flush against the surface of the wider board. Slide a narrow strip of scrap up to the leading edge of the crown molding as it rests on the wide jig board. Be careful not to dislodge the crown molding. Mark the position of the narrow strip, then fasten it to the wide jig board with screws.

To make a 45° miter cut, simply set your crown molding into the jig as shown, swivel your miter saw to 45° and make the cut. Be sure to use the inside dimensions of the crown molding when measuring.

36 Attach the crown molding to the scrap wood frame with glue and 4d finish nails driven into pilot holes. Drive a finish nail into each miter joint to lock the joint together. Set all the nails below the surface with a nailset.

37 Drill screw slots in the molding frame to attach it to the cabinet top the same way the base is attached to the lower cabinet. Attach the crown molding assembly to the top of the cabinet, using #8 × 1¼-in. wood screws with washers **(See Photo T).**

APPLY FINISHING TOUCHES
38 Rip-cut scraps of your red oak stock into ¼ × ⅜-in. strips to make the glass retainer strips (you'll need about 22 lineal ft.).

39 Fill all nail holes with stainable wood putty, then finish-sand all wood parts to 180-grit, easing any sharp edges as you work. Wipe the surfaces clean with a tack cloth, then apply your finish (we used medium walnut stain and tung oil).

40 Set the glass panels into the recesses in the cabinet doors, then attach the retainer strips on the inside of each recess, using 1-in. wire nails, to hold the panels in place **(See Photo U).** Install the door hinges, pulls and catches. Screw the lower cabinet to the upper cabinet **(See Photo V).**

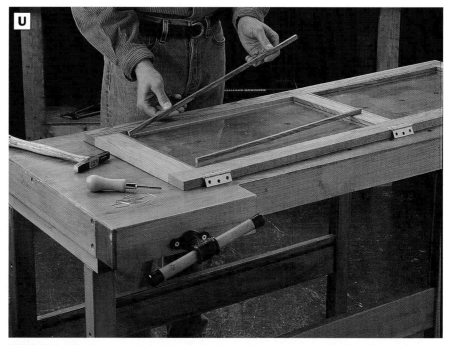

PHOTO U: Set the glass panels in place in the doors and secure them with ¼ × ⅜-in. oak retainer strips. Use 1-in. wire brads driven into pilot holes to fasten the strips to the inside edges of the rabbet grooves in the door frames.

PHOTO V: Screw the upper and lower cabinets together. Lay the cabinets down so their backs are flush. Center the upper cabinet on the lower cabinet, side to side, and hold them tightly together. Drill countersink holes for the screws (a tapered countersink hole will allow the screws to draw the parts together tightly).

Colonial Step Stool

Take a step back in time by building this practical step stool. Based on a traditional Colonial bench design, this solid and sturdy companion for the kitchen or bathroom is made almost exclusively with hand tools and traditional woodworking techniques. The keyed tenons on the single spreader, the simple scallops and gentle splay of the legs, and the solid hardwood construction are the elements that give the stool a sense of character and history. For added effect, we distressed the wood surfaces to lend an antique flavor to this faithful reproduction.

Vital Statistics: Colonial Step Stool

TYPE: Step stool

OVERALL SIZE: 18W by 12H by 10D

MATERIAL: Ash

JOINERY: Dowel joints, keyed mortise-and-tenons (pinned)

CONSTRUCTION DETAILS:

· Legs and top are made from 10-in.-wide-boards (solid or edge-glued)

· All parts are cut and shaped with hand tools, including a coping saw (leg contours) and a draw knife (spreader)

· Legs splay inward at 10° angle

· Keys at ends of spreader are pinned with dowels

· Wood surfaces are distressed

FINISHING OPTIONS: For an antique look, use a medium to dark wood stain, followed by a low-gloss (satin) topcoat. As shown, the stool is finished with maple stain and three coats of satin tung oil.

Building time

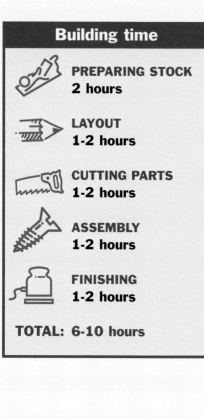

PREPARING STOCK
2 hours

LAYOUT
1-2 hours

CUTTING PARTS
1-2 hours

ASSEMBLY
1-2 hours

FINISHING
1-2 hours

TOTAL: 6-10 hours

Tools you'll use

· Cross-cut saw

· Ripping saw

· Back saw or tenon saw

· Coping saw

· Drill

· No.5 jack plane

· Block plane

· Draw knife

· Wood mallet

· Strap clamp

· Combination square

· Wood chisels

· Woodscrews or C-clamps

· Drill guide

· Heavy chain (optional)

Shopping list

☐ (3) ¾ × 4 in. × 6 ft. ash boards

☐ (1) 1½ × 1½ × at least 24 in. ash board

☐ (8) ⅜ in.-dia.-wood dowel (hardwood)

☐ (2) ⅛ in. dia. wood dowel (hardwood)

☐ Finishing materials

Colonial Step Stool

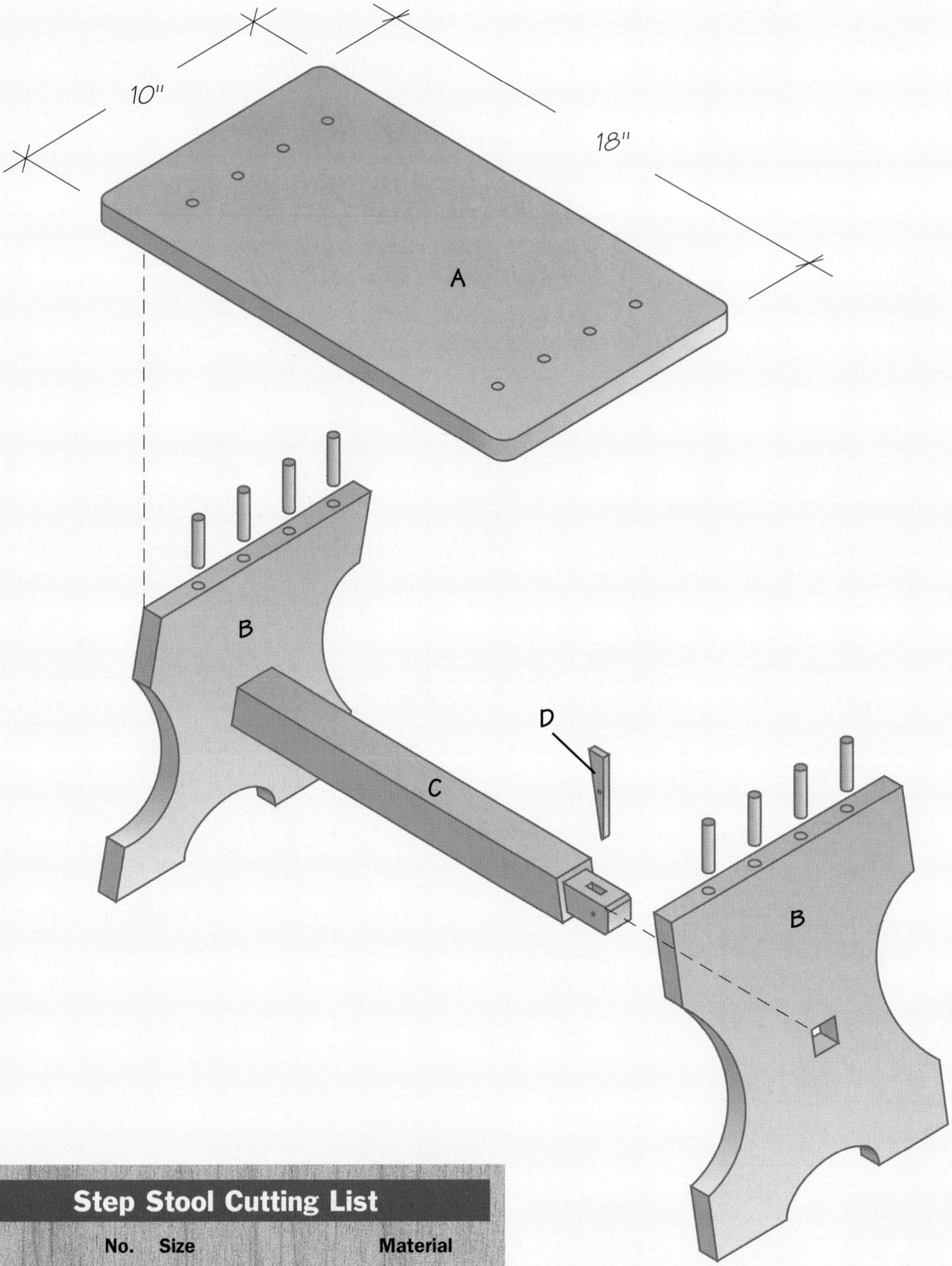

A

10"

18"

B

C

D

B

Step Stool Cutting List			
Part	**No.**	**Size**	**Material**
A. Top	1	¾ × 10 × 18 in.	Ash
B. Legs	2	¾ × 10 × 11⅜ in.	"
C. Stretcher	1	1½ × 1½ × 18 in.	"
D. Keys	2	¼ × ⅝ × 3 in.	"

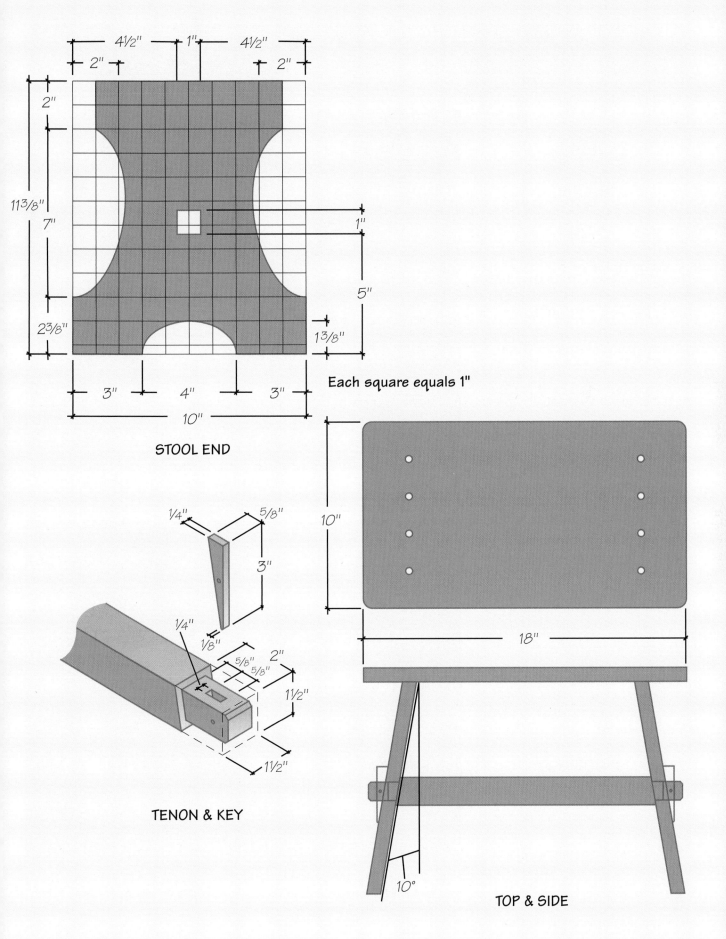

STOOL END

4½" 1" 4½"
2" 2"
2"
11³⁄₈"
7"
1"
2³⁄₈" 1³⁄₈" 5"
3" 4" 3"
10"

Each square equals 1"

TENON & KEY

¼" 5⁄₈"
3"
¼"
1⁄₈"
5⁄₈" 2"
5⁄₈"
1½"
1½"

TOP & SIDE

10"
18"
10°

MAKE THE LEGS & TOP

In Colonial times, it was not difficult to find lumber wide enough to build furniture with 10-in.-wide or larger parts without the need for edge-gluing stock to width. But today, it's likely that you'll need to glue up boards to make the top and legs for this step stool.

1 Select enough lumber to make the blanks for the top and legs (if you use boards at least 42 in. long, you can cut all three parts from one glued-up panel). Plane the boards to thickness, then joint one edge of each board using a power jointer or a jointing plane. Rip-cut the boards to width, then joint the sawn edge of each board. Edge-glue the boards to make your panel, using dowels or biscuits to align the boards and reinforce the glue joints. After the glue cures, smooth out the seams, as needed, using a plane, power planer, cabinet scraper or sander **(See Photo A).**

2 Cross-cut all three parts to length (we used a hand saw in keeping with our "traditional" approach to building this project). Round over the corners of the top with a hand file or block plane. Ease the sharp edges all around.

3 Set a sliding T-bevel gauge to 10° and mark the angle on the

PHOTO A: Secure the board you'll use to make the tops and legs to your workbench, then plane the surface with a No. 5 jack plane to level the edge-glued joints. A power planer can also be used for this task. Plane in diagonal strokes with the grain.

Backup board

PHOTO B: Plane parallel 10° bevels in the top and bottom edge of each leg with a block plane. A backup board the same thickness as the workpiece will keep the side grain of the wood from splitting off at the end of the planing stroke.

 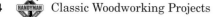

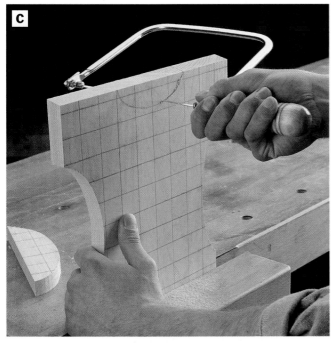

PHOTO C: Transfer the leg pattern onto one leg and cut the contours with a coping saw. File the cuts smooth, then use the leg as a template to trace the pattern onto the other leg.

PHOTO D: Make the cheek and shoulder cuts for the tenons at the ends of the spreader with a sharp back saw. Make sure the shoulder cuts follow the 10° angle of the leg bevels.

sides of both ends of the legs. Square the lines across the faces. Using these lines as guides, bevel the top and bottom of each leg at 10°—we used a hand plane **(See Photo B).**

4 Draw a grid pattern on one of the legs and transfer the shape from the *Grid pattern* shown on page 53 onto the workpiece. Cut the contours with a coping saw, cutting carefully along the waste side of the lines **(See Photo C).** Smooth out the contours with a file or rasp, then trace the contours onto the other leg. Cut the second leg, then ease all the sharp edges of both legs (except the top edges).

5 Cut a 1-in. square mortise in each leg for the stretcher. Draw outlines, then drill an entry hole and make the cutout with a coping saw. The bottom of each mortise should be 5 in. up from the bottom of the leg. The top and bottom of each mortise should be parallel to the top and bottom of each leg end (this means they will be angled at 10°, rather than square, to the faces). Smooth the cuts and square the corners with a file.

MAKE THE STRETCHER

6 Cut the stretcher to length (18 in.) from a piece of 1½- × 1½-in. ash. With a bevel gauge, mark 10° shoulder cuts on the front and back faces. Start the shoulder cut at the maximum distance of 2 in. in

PHOTO E: Use a sharp chisel to square off the mortises in the tops of the spreader tenons. Use a drill to remove most of the waste. These tapered mortises will accept the keys used to pin the mortise-and-tenon joints that secure the spreader and the legs.

PHOTO F: Shape the edges of the spreader with chamfers to give it a more rustic appearance. We used a draw knife, but you could also use a spoke shave or a hand plane for a hand-hewn look.

PHOTO G: Use a strap clamp to draw the top tight against the tops of the legs while the glue dries. Double-check your reference lines to make sure the top is centered properly.

from each end, and angle it back from there, as shown in the *Tenon & key diagram* on page 53. Square the lines across the top and bottom faces. Set a marking or cutting gauge to ¼ in. and outline the tenon on the ends of the stretcher. Continue the lines back

PHOTO H: Drill 10° dowel holes through the top and into the centers of the legs. We used a drilling guide to set the drilling angle and the 1½-in. drilling depth.

to the shoulders on the top and bottom faces only.

7 Make the angled shoulder cuts ¼ in. deep with a back saw, with the stretcher clamped horizontally in a vise. Then clamp it vertically and cut straight down along the waste sides of the cheek lines to the shoulders. The waste pieces will fall off.

8 With the marking gauge, mark the ¼-in. cutting lines for the tops and bottoms of the tenons along the faces of the cheeks you've just cut. Make shoulder cuts and cheek cuts (**See Photo D**). Clean up the surfaces and corners with a file. Test the fit in the mortises and adjust as necessary.

9 Cut mortises for the keys in the ends of the stretcher. The mortises should be ¼ in. wide and centered along the thickness of the tenons. Make them ⅝ in. long at the top, but taper the inside end of each mortise so it's parallel

with the shoulder. Mark the top and bottom of each mortise by drawing lines around the tenon with a square and bevel gauge. Remove waste with a drill, then square the edges with a chisel (**See Photo E**).

10 Clamp the stretcher firmly and chamfer the edges with a Draw knife or a hand plane (**See Photo F**). Make several light passes rather than trying to do the chamfer in one cut.

ASSEMBLE THE STOOL
11 Cut two keys 3 in. long, ⅝ in. wide, and ¼ in. thick. Trim the keys so they taper from ⅝ in. at the top to ⅛ in. at the bottom. Round over the square corner at the wide end of each key.

12 Dry-assemble the legs and stretcher, tapping the keys gently into place. Set the assembly on a flat surface and make sure it is square and level. Adjust the joints as needed. Don't glue it together

PHOTO I: Drive ⅜- × 2-in. dowels into the dowel holes to reinforce the joints between the top and the legs. Apply glue to the ends of the dowels before inserting. Trim the exposed dowel ends flush with the top.

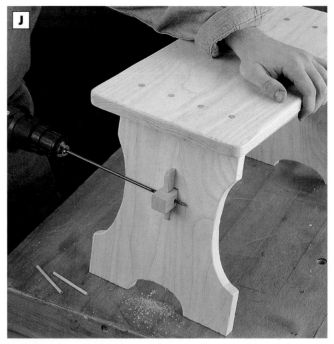

PHOTO J: Use an extended bit to drill ⅛-in.-dia. holes through the spreader tenons and each key, then pin the tenons into the mortises with ⅛-in.-dia. dowels.

yet. Set the top onto the assembly and center it so there is an equal overhang at both ends, and at the front and back. Mark the position of the legs on the underside of the top.

⓭ Apply glue to the tops of the legs, put the top in position, and clamp it down to the legs with a strap clamp (**See Photo G).**

⓮ After the glue cures, remove the strap clamp and mark two lines across the top, centered along the tops of the legs. Mark four evenly spaced drilling points along each line, then drill 10° guide holes for dowels at each drilling point, using a ⅜-in.-dia. bit set to drill 1½ in. deep (**See Photo H).** The dowel holes should stay centered in the legs.

⓯ Cut eight ⅜-in. hardwood dowels to a length of 2 in., then apply glue and drive them into the dowel holes with a wood mallet (**See Photo I).** Trim the ends of the dowels with a flush-cutting saw and sand or plane them flush with the surface of the top.

⓰ Drill a ⅛-in.-dia. guide hole through each tenon key for a ⅛-in. dowel pin. Center the holes on the keys. This will be easiest to do with an extended drill bit (**See Photo J).** Drive ⅛-in. hardwood dowels through the guide holes to pin the keys in place. Trim the ends of the pins with a flush-cutting saw.

PHOTO K (OPTION): For an antiqued appearance, distress the wood surfaces with a chain or ring of car keys before applying the finish.

APPLY FINISHING TOUCHES

⓱ Finish-sand all surfaces with 150-, then 180-grit sandpaper. For an antiqued appearance, we decided to distress the stool before applying the finish. There are many ways to accomplish this. We elected to rake a piece of heavy chain across the top and the outside faces of the legs (**See Photo K).** For a finish, we used maple stain with a tung oil topcoat.

Picnic Table & Benches

This unusual picnic table and bench set combines the look of traditional picnic table styling with the space-efficiency of a round table. With the 58-in.-dia. top and four long benches, as many as eight adults can enjoy dining in the great outdoors using this lovely set.

Vital Statistics: Picnic Table & Benches

TYPE: Round cross-buck picnic table with curved benches

OVERALL SIZE: 58-in.-dia. by 30H (table)

17H by 41¾W by 12¾D (bench)

MATERIAL: Dimensional cedar

JOINERY: Half-lap joints and butt joints reinforced with carriage bolts and galvanized deck screws

CONSTRUCTION DETAILS:

· Spacious round tabletop seats up to eight adults

· Traditional cross-buck look on legs

· Alternating board width on tabletop and benchtop

· No planing or jointing required

FINISHING OPTIONS: Clear, UV-resistant topcoat (exterior wood stain optional), or leave untreated for natural gray look.

Building time (table)

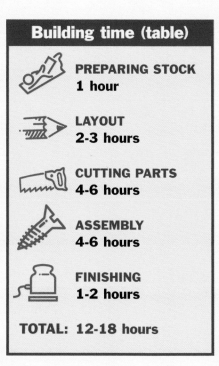

PREPARING STOCK
1 hour

LAYOUT
2-3 hours

CUTTING PARTS
4-6 hours

ASSEMBLY
4-6 hours

FINISHING
1-2 hours

TOTAL: 12-18 hours

Tools you'll use

· Straightedge cutting guide

· C-clamps

· Router with ⅜-in. roundover bit

· Table saw with dado-blade set

· Tape measure

· 64-in. or longer bar or pipe clamps (2)

· Spring clamps

· Jig saw or band saw

· Combination square

· Framing (carpenter's) square

· Drill/driver

Shopping list

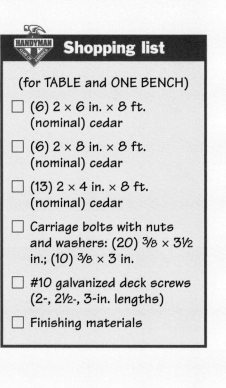

(for TABLE and ONE BENCH)

☐ (6) 2 × 6 in. × 8 ft. (nominal) cedar

☐ (6) 2 × 8 in. × 8 ft. (nominal) cedar

☐ (13) 2 × 4 in. × 8 ft. (nominal) cedar

☐ Carriage bolts with nuts and washers: (20) ⅜ × 3½ in.; (10) ⅜ × 3 in.

☐ #10 galvanized deck screws (2-, 2½-, 3-in. lengths)

☐ Finishing materials

Picnic Table & Benches

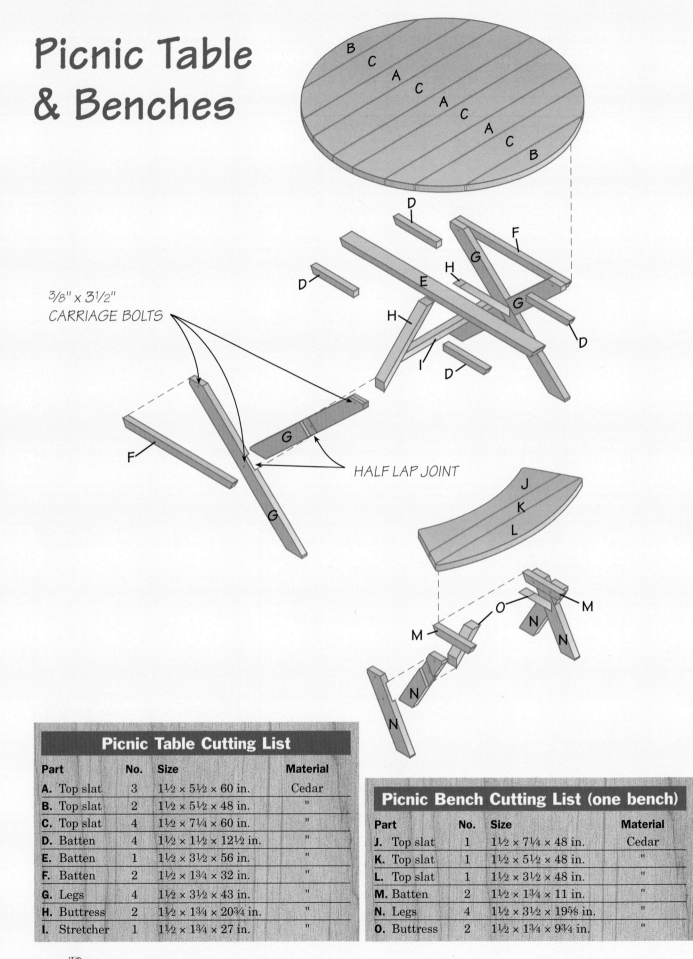

3/8" x 3½"
CARRIAGE BOLTS

HALF LAP JOINT

Picnic Table Cutting List

Part		No.	Size	Material
A.	Top slat	3	1½ × 5½ × 60 in.	Cedar
B.	Top slat	2	1½ × 5½ × 48 in.	"
C.	Top slat	4	1½ × 7¼ × 60 in.	"
D.	Batten	4	1½ × 1½ × 12½ in.	"
E.	Batten	1	1½ × 3½ × 56 in.	"
F.	Batten	2	1½ × 1¾ × 32 in.	"
G.	Legs	4	1½ × 3½ × 43 in.	"
H.	Buttress	2	1½ × 1¾ × 20¾ in.	"
I.	Stretcher	1	1½ × 1¾ × 27 in.	"

Picnic Bench Cutting List (one bench)

Part		No.	Size	Material
J.	Top slat	1	1½ × 7¼ × 48 in.	Cedar
K.	Top slat	1	1½ × 5½ × 48 in.	"
L.	Top slat	1	1½ × 3½ × 48 in.	"
M.	Batten	2	1½ × 1¾ × 11 in.	"
N.	Legs	4	1½ × 3½ × 19⅝ in.	"
O.	Buttress	2	1½ × 1¾ × 9¾ in.	"

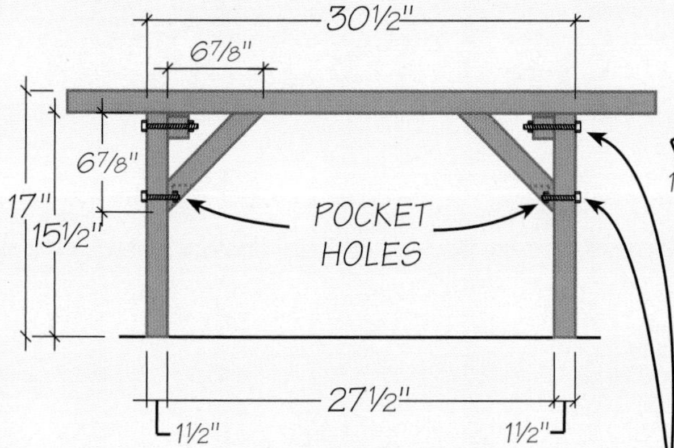
30 1/2"
6 7/8"
6 7/8"
17"
15 1/2"
POCKET HOLES
27 1/2"
1 1/2"
1 1/2"
3/8" x 3 1/2" CARRIAGE BOLTS

FRONT ELEVATION (BENCH)

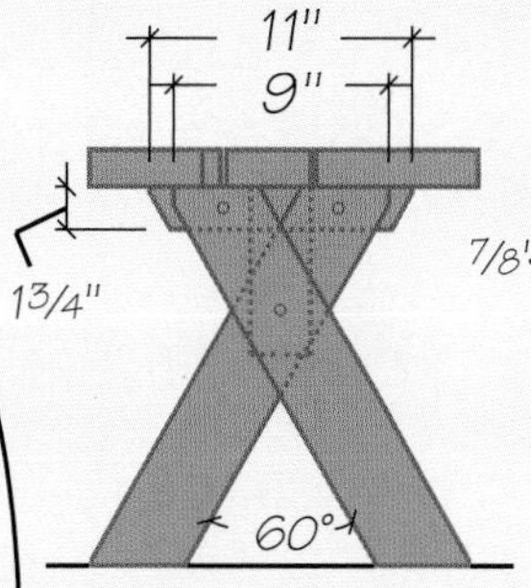
11"
9"
1 3/4"
60°

SIDE ELEVATION (BENCH)

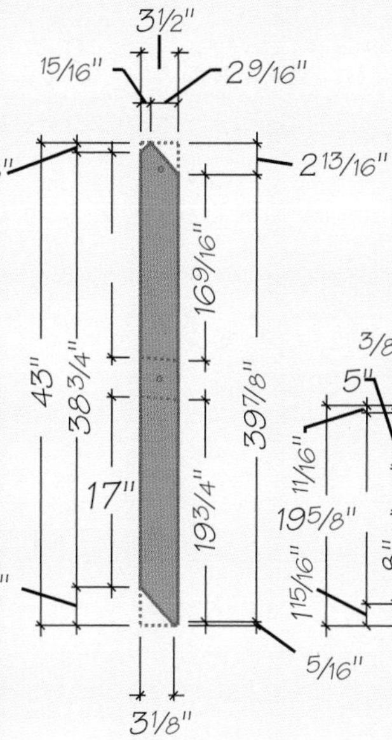
3 1/2"
15/16"
2 9/16"
7/8"
2 13/16"
16 9/16"
43"
38 3/4"
39 7/8"
17"
19 3/4"
3 3/8"
5/16"
3 1/8"

TABLE LEG

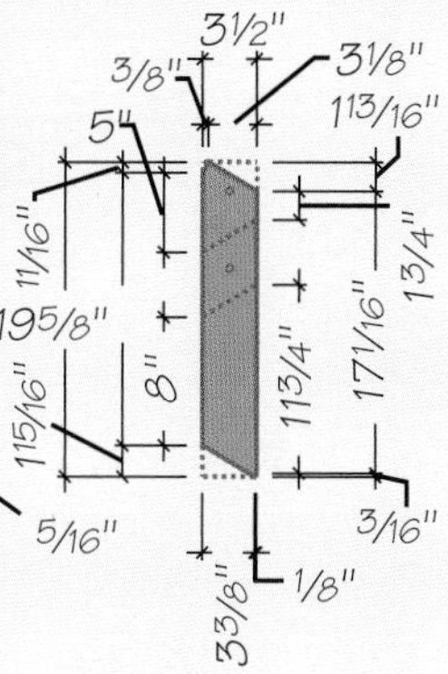
3 1/2"
3/8"
3 1/8"
5"
1 13/16"
1 1/16"
1 3/4"
19 5/8"
8"
11 3/4"
17 1/16"
1 15/16"
3/16"
1/8"
3 3/8"

BENCH LEG

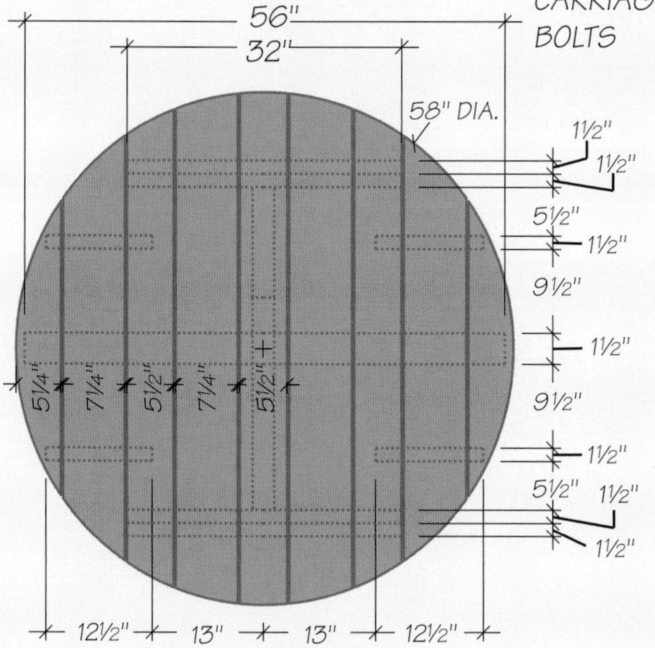
56"
32"
58" DIA.
1 1/2"
1 1/2"
5 1/2"
1 1/2"
9 1/2"
1 1/2"
9 1/2"
1 1/2"
5 1/2"
1 1/2"
1 1/2"
5 1/4"
7 1/4"
5 1/2"
7 1/4"
5 1/2"
12 1/2"
13"
13"
12 1/2"

TOP VIEW (TABLE)

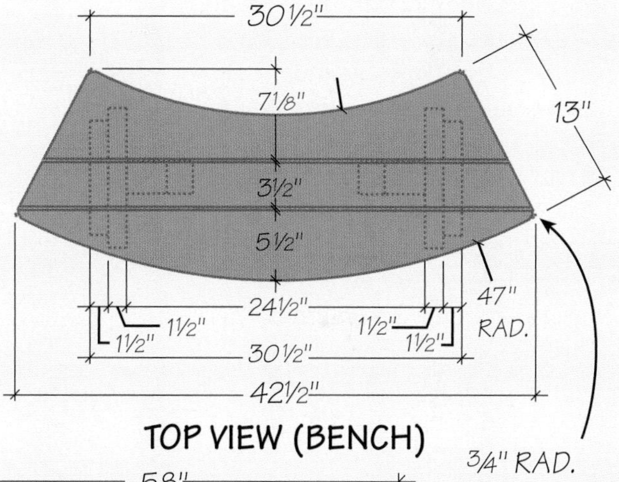
30 1/2"
13"
7 1/8"
3 1/2"
5 1/2"
24 1/2"
1 1/2"
1 1/2"
1 1/2"
1 1/2"
30 1/2"
47" RAD.
42 1/2"
3/4" RAD.

TOP VIEW (BENCH)

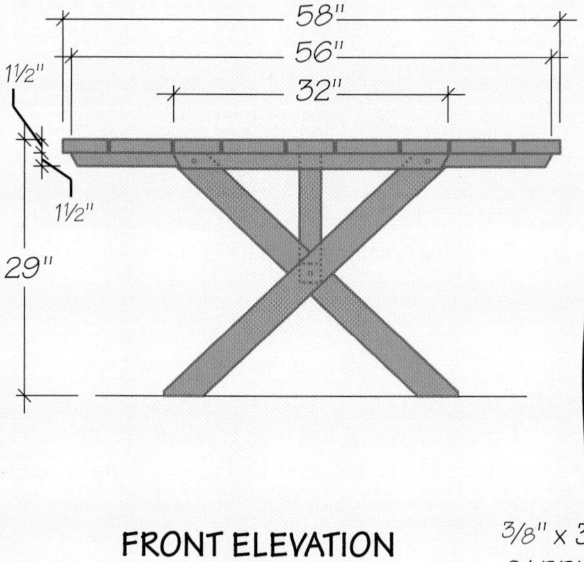
58"
56"
32"
1 1/2"
1 1/2"
29"

FRONT ELEVATION (TABLE)

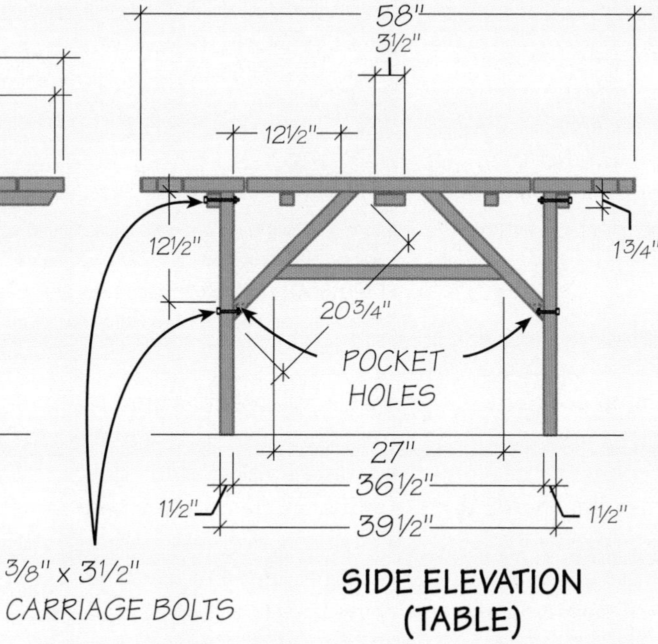
58"
3 1/2"
12 1/2"
12 1/2"
1 3/4"
20 3/4"
POCKET HOLES
27"
36 1/2"
39 1/2"
1 1/2"
1 1/2"
3/8" x 3 1/2" CARRIAGE BOLTS

SIDE ELEVATION (TABLE)

PHOTO A: Lay out the boards with the tabletop facing down. Separate the boards with ¼-in. spacers and clamp the setup together. Draw two perpendicular centerlines, and use a trammel to swing a 29-in.-radius circle from the point where the two lines intersect.

MAKE THE TABLETOP

The round top for this picnic table is cut from nine 2× cedar boards laid edge-to edge. The layout alternates between 5½-in.-wide boards (nominal 2 × 6) and 7¼ in.-wide boards (nominal 2 × 8) for an interesting pattern that, when added to the ¼-in. gap between boards, results in a tabletop that has a generous diameter of 58 in.

1 Cut the nine boards for the tabletop to the lengths listed in the *Cutting list* on page 60. Select a 60-in.-long 2 × 6 and draw a centerline along the length of the board to mark the center of the tabletop. Use a combination square and pencil to draw the centerline. Lay out the boards in the order shown in *Top view (Table)* on page 61, positioning the board with the centerline in the middle of the layout. Insert spacers made from ¼-in.-thick scrap between the boards, then draw the boards together with a pipe clamp near each end of the layout.

2 Draw a centerline perpendicular to the first centerline. Measure to find the midpoints of the two end boards to mark endpoints for the second centerline. Lay a straightedge across the boards to mark the line, but check with a framing square first to make sure the centerlines are perpendicular.

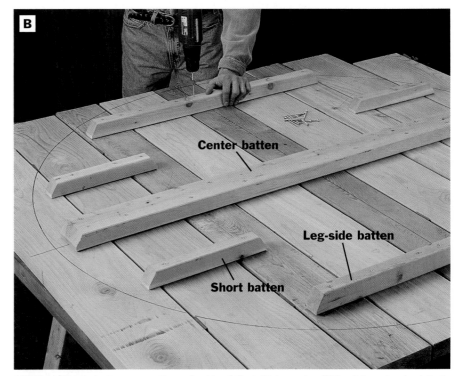

PHOTO B: Attach the battens to the underside of the tabletop using #10 × 2 in. galvanized deck screws for the short battens and the center batten. Use 2½-in. screws for the leg-side battens.

3 Use the point where the two lines intersect as a centerpoint for scribing a 58-in.-dia. (29-in.-radius) circle onto the boards **(See Photo A).** We used a shop-built trammel made of hardboard to draw the circle (See page 110).

4 Cut the seven battens to size. Cross-cut the center batten to 56 in. from a 2 × 4, and cut the four short battens to 12½ in. long from 2 × 2 stock. Rip the leg-side battens to 1¾ in. wide from a 2 × 3 or 2 × 4, then cross-cut them to 32 in.

 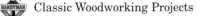

PHOTO C: Round over the top and bottom edges of the tabletop with a router and ⅜-in. roundover bit. Move clockwise around the tabletop.

PHOTO D: Cut half-laps into the legs with a dado-blade set. Make multiple passes, using a miter gauge set at 85° to guide the stock.

⑤ Make a 60° trim cut at the end of each batten, starting ¼ in. down from the face of the batten that will contact the underside of the table. The trim cuts serve to eliminate the sharp ends. Make the trim cuts on a power miter saw. *NOTE: The battens that attach to the legs are installed with the 1½ in. edge up against the tabletop, so be sure your trim cuts are on the correct faces.*

⑥ Mark the midpoint of the center batten's length, and square the line all around the board. Now measure 1¾ in. on either side of the second (cross-grain) centerline on the tabletop and lay the center batten on these marks, aligning the midpoint line on the batten with the centerline along the center board of the tabletop.

⑦ Drill countersunk pilot holes, then attach the center batten to the tabletop boards with #10 × 2-in. galvanized deck screws. Position the remaining battens on the underside of the tabletop, as shown in *Top view (Table)* on page 61, and attach with screws (**See Photo B**).

⑧ Cut out the circle along the waste side of the line with a jig saw. Smooth out any unevenness in the cut with a power sander.

⑨ Install a piloted ⅜-in. roundover bit (See *FYI*, right) in your router and round the top and bottom edges of the tabletop (**See Photo C**).

MAKE & ATTACH THE TABLE LEGS

⑩ Lay out and cut the four table legs from 2 × 4 cedar. Use the measurements shown in the drawing on page 61 as a reference for scribing the layout lines. Cut the parallel, angled ends and the 90° tip cutoffs on the table saw or power miter saw.

⑪ Lay out the half-lap joints cut into the legs in the positions indicated on the drawing.

⑫ We used a dado-blade set mounted in our table saw to remove the wood in the half-lap joint areas. Set the blade to its widest cutting width, then raise it to a ¾-in. cutting depth. Set the miter gauge on your table saw to 85°, and feed each leg over the

ROUNDOVER BITS

Piloted roundover bits, like the ⅜-in. roundover bit shown above, cut smooth, even curves into edges of boards. Rounded edges increase safety and visual appeal. Other examples of edge-profiling bits are chamfer bits and ogee bits, seen elsewhere in this book.

blade in multiple passes to remove the wood in the joint areas (**See Photo D**).

⑬ Put the half-laps together to assemble the legs. Clamp the joints temporarily to stabilize them. Then position the leg assemblies in place against the

PHOTO E: Clamp the legs together and drill clearance holes for carriage bolts through the battens and legs. Keep the drill level.

PHOTO F: Drill clearance holes for ⅜ × 3½-in. carriage bolts through the end of each buttress, then through the half-lap leg joint.

PHOTO G: Screw the buttresses to the tabletop. Use a square to maintain a perpendicular angle between the leg assembly and the tabletop.

leg-side battens. Align the ends of the leg tops flush with the ends of the battens.

14 Clamp the legs to the battens (along with a scrap backup board to prevent drilling tearout), and drill clearance holes for ⅜ × 3½-in. carriage bolts through the battens and the leg tops, in the positions shown on page 60 **(See Photo E).**

15 Insert the 3½-in. carriage bolts from the outside, and secure the legs to the battens with washers and nuts fastened to the bolts.

INSTALL THE TABLE LEG SUPPORTS

The table legs receive lateral support from a pair of buttresses and a spreader that form a center brace assembly.

16 Rip-cut 2 × 4 or 2 × 3 stock to 1¾ in. wide. Cut the angled buttresses to length, making 45° miter cuts at the ends. The buttresses should be 20¾ in. long at their longest points. Cut the center stretcher to size, mitering the ends so it's 27 in. long at it's longest point.

17 Measure up 12½ in. from the underside of the tabletop and make a mark on the inside juncture of each leg assembly. Mark the center of the width on one end of each buttress. Measure across the juncture of the leg assembly and mark a midpoint, then extend it vertically with a carpenter's square. Hold a buttress in place against one of the leg assemblies, with the lower edge of its upper miter at the height mark, and the centerlines on the buttress and leg assemblies aligned. Drill a pocket hole into the buttress, then follow with a clearance hole for a carriage bolt, keeping the drill level **(See Photo F).** Bolt the buttress to the legs with ⅜ × 3½-in. carriage bolts. Repeat for the other side.

18 Drill countersunk pilot holes and screw the free ends of the buttresses to the underside of the tabletop **(See Photo G).** To make sure the buttresses are in the right position and the legs are perpendicular to the top, hold a carpenter's square up against each leg as you attach it.

19 Put the center stretcher in place across the buttresses. Place a level on the stretcher and adjust it until it's level. Then drill angled pilot holes and screw the stretcher to the buttresses with #10 × 2-in. deck screws **(See Photo H).**

BUILD THE BENCHES

The following instructions, the *Shopping List* on page 59 and the *Cutting List* on page 60 all provide information for building one bench only. If you want to build four of the curved benches to complete the outdoor dining set, multiply the quantities for the bench parts by four to calculate your shopping list. Much of the assembly sequence for the benches repeats techniques used to make the table. Refer to the above sections for more information if you're unsure about any steps in the bench-construction process.

20 Lay out the boards for the benchtop with ¼-in. spacers between them and stabilize the setup with clamps. Draw the outline of the benchtop shape onto the boards, using the measurements and arc radii shown in the illustrations on page 61. (If you're planning to build all four benches, it would be worth your while to make a template for the benchtops.)

21 Rip-cut one edge of the batten stock and cut the battens to length. Cut the angled ends the same as those on the table battens.

22 Screw the battens to the underside of the top, 24½ in. apart and positioned as shown in the illustration on page 61.

23 Cut the benchtop to shape with a jig saw **(See Photo I),** and round the corners with a ¾-in. radius, using your jig saw. Smooth the edges, then run a router with a ⅜-in. roundover bit around the edges as before.

24 Cut the legs and buttresses to size. Lay out and cut the leg half-laps using the same methods you did on the table legs, but use a 60° angle instead of 85°.

25 Assemble the leg structure as before. Follow the same steps for bolting the legs to the battens, and for attaching the buttresses **(See Photo J).**

26 Sand the wood lightly to smooth out any rough or splintered surfaces.

27 Use an exterior stain to seal and protect the wood. Alternatively it can be painted or left to age gracefully to an elegant silver-gray (cedar and redwood are highly weather-resistant).

PHOTO H: Attach the ends of the stretcher to the buttresses with two #10 × 2-in. deck screws at each joint. Make sure the stretcher is level.

PHOTO I: After the battens have been attached, cut out the shape of the benchtop with a jig saw.

PHOTO J: Attach the bench buttresses as you did the table buttresses, using a square to keep the legs perpendicular.

Toy Chest

Smart joinery and a sleek design come together in this creative kids' project. The sturdy sliding lids eliminate pinching and slamming but can still put up with all the climbing and jumping your special child can inflict on them. Add some fun finishing, like the jaunty, multi-colored painting scheme used above, and the result is a unique toy chest that can be passed along from generation to generation.

Vital Statistics: Toy Chest

TYPE: Toy chest

OVERALL SIZE: 36W by 18H by 20D

MATERIAL: Poplar and birch plywood

JOINERY: Tongue-and-groove joints

CONSTRUCTION DETAILS:

· Tracked, sliding lids on top eliminate pinch points
· Sturdy ½-in. plywood construction withstands abuse
· Frame-and-panel sides, front, and back give chest unique appeal
· Bottom panel supported by hardwood cleats

FINISHING OPTIONS: Paint with durable child-safe enamel paint, using primary colors or a combination of bright tones.

Building time

PREPARING STOCK
2 hours

LAYOUT
2-4 hours

CUTTING PARTS
3-5 hours

ASSEMBLY
3-5 hours

FINISHING
2-4 hours

TOTAL: 12-20 hours

Tools you'll use

· Table saw
· Straightedge cutting guide
· C-clamps or spring clamps
· Router (or router table) with piloted ¼-in. roundover bit and ⅝-in. straight bit
· Tape measure/metal rule
· 36-in. or longer bar or pipe clamps (8)
· Jig saw or band saw
· Drill/driver
· Wood mallet
· Dado-blade set for table saw
· Tenoning jig

Shopping list

☐ (1) ½ × 4 × 8 sheet cabinet-grade birch plywood

☐ (2) ⁵⁄4 or ⁶⁄4 × 8 in. × 8 ft. clear poplar or other inexpensive hardwood

☐ (2) ¾ × 1 × 16 in. strips of maple or other decorative hardwood.

☐ Wallboard screws (1 in., 1⅝ in.)

☐ ¼-in. hardwood doweling

☐ Wood glue

☐ Finishing materials

Toy Chest

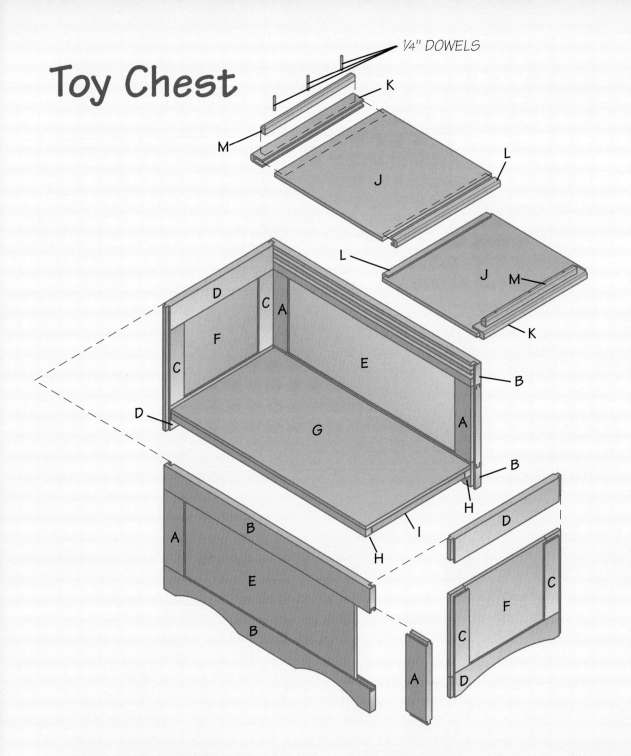

¼" DOWELS

K

M

J

L

L

J

M

K

D

C

A

F

E

C

B

D

A

B

G

H

B

H

I

A

B

E

B

D

F

C

C

H

A

D

Toy Chest Cutting List

Part	No.	Size	Material	Part	No.	Size	Material
A. Stiles (front/back)	4	4/4 × 3½ × 12 in.	Poplar	**G.** Panel (bottom)	1	½ × 18 × 34 in.	Birch plywood
B. Rails (front/back)	4	4/4 × 3½ × 36 in.	"	**H.** Long cleats	2	4/4 × 4/4 × 34 in.	Any hardwood
C. Stiles (side)	4	4/4 × 3 × 12 in.	"	**I.** Short cleats	2	4/4 × 4/4 × 15¾ in.	"
D. Rails (side)	4	4/4 × 3½ × 19 in.	"	**J.** Lid panels	2	½ × 18¾ × 16¼ in.	Birch plywood
E. Panels (front/back)	2	½ × 12 × 30 in.	Birch plywood	**K.** Lid caps	2	4/4 × 2 × 17¾ in.	Poplar
				L. Lid ends	2	4/4 × 4/4 × 17¾ in.	"
F. Panels (side)	2	½ × 12 × 14 in.	"	**M.** Lid pulls	2	¾ × 4/4 × 15¾ in.	"

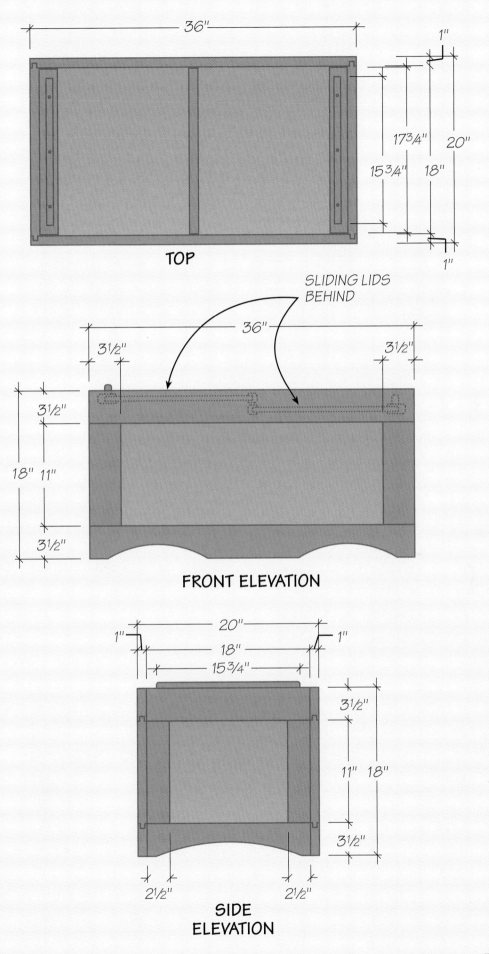

TOP

SLIDING LIDS BEHIND

FRONT ELEVATION

SIDE ELEVATION

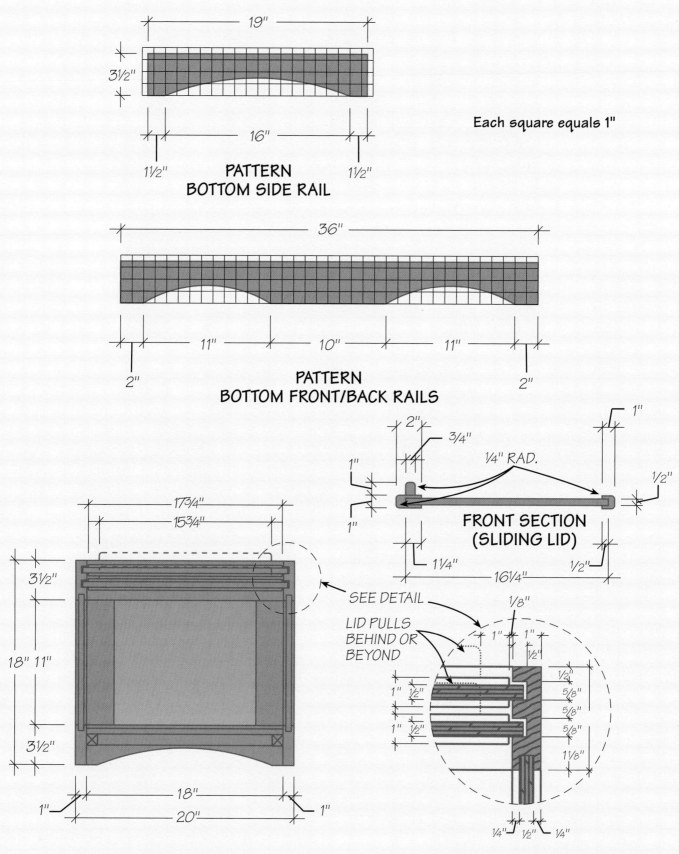

19"

3½"

16"

1½"   1½"

**PATTERN
BOTTOM SIDE RAIL**

Each square equals 1"

36"

11"   10"   11"

2"   2"

**PATTERN
BOTTOM FRONT/BACK RAILS**

2"

3/4"

1"   1/4" RAD.   1"

1"   1/2"

1"

**FRONT SECTION
(SLIDING LID)**

1¼"   1/2"

16¼"   1/2"

17¾"

15¾"

3½"

SEE DETAIL

LID PULLS
BEHIND OR
BEYOND

1/8"

18" 11"

1" 1"

1/2"

1" 1/2"   1/2"

5/8"

5/8"

1" 1/2"

5/8"

3½"

1" 1/2"

1 1/8"

18"

1"   20"   1"

1/4" 1/2" 1/4"

SIDE SECTION

DETAIL AT SLIDING LIDS

MAKE THE CHEST PANELS

The carcase for this toy chest features four frame-and-panel assemblies joined with tongue-and-groove joints. The rails and stiles are grooved along the inside edges to accept the ½-in. plywood panel inserts, and the ends of the stiles are tenoned to fit into the ends of the rail grooves. Tongue-and-groove joints used to connect the front and back to the sides, forming the chest carcase, and also the slots in the top rails that hold the sliding chest lids, are cut after the framed panels are assembled.

❶ Plane two 8-ft.-long by 4-in.-wide ⁶⁄₄ or ⁵⁄₄ poplar boards (depending upon lumberyard availability) to ⁴⁄₄ (1 in.) thickness to prepare the stock for the rails and stiles used to make the chest panels. Flatten and square one edge of each board on the jointer.

❷ With the jointed edges against the table saw fence, rip-cut each board to 3½ in. wide. Cross-cut eight lengths to 12 in. long for all the stiles. Cross-cut four lengths to 36 in. (the front and back rails) and four to 19 in. (the side rails). Rip-cut four of the stiles down to 3 in., as the side stiles are narrower.

❸ Cut the ½ × ½-in. dadoes for the panel inserts. We used a table saw with a dado-blade set adjusted to a ½-in. cutting width and set to ½-in. cutting height. Set the rip fence on your table saw ¼ in. away from the cutters on the dado-blade set. Cut a dado into the inside edge of each rail and stile (See **Photo A**).

❹ Cut tenons on both ends of the stiles, using your table saw (replace the dado-blade set with a combination blade). First, clamp each stile on-end to a table saw tenoning jig and make the cheek cuts on both sides to create a ½-in.-thick × ½-in.-long tenon (See **Photo B**). Make practice cuts on scrap stock to

PHOTO A: Cut a ½ × ½-in. dado in one long edge of each rail and stile, using a dado-blade set mounted in your table saw. Adjust the rip fence so the dado is centered on the edge of the workpiece.

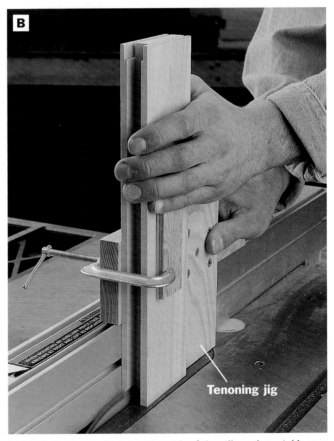

Tenoning jig

PHOTO B: Cut tenon cheeks on the ends of the stiles using a table saw tenon jig. The jig shown above is made from two pieces of scrap joined in a "T" configuration so a vertical piece rides on the table while a horizontal piece rides on the rip fence. Clamp the workpiece to the jig.

PHOTO C: Make shoulder cuts on your table saw to trim off the waste around each tenon. Butt the workpiece against a relief block clamped to the rip fence to index the cut. Keep the relief block fully on the infeed side of the blade distanced at least the width of the stock away.

PHOTO D: Draw the contours for the scallops on lower chest rails so the scallops face the undadoed edge. We created a full-size template from hardboard for each shape.

PHOTO E: Assemble the frame-and-panel sides, front and back for the chest. Glue the tenons in the stiles into the grooves in the rails, but do not glue the inserted plywood panels into the grooves—they can float freely in the rail and stile frames. Use scrap wood cauls between the clamp jaws and the chest frames to keep the jaws from marring the wood.

be sure the tenons fit tightly into the dadoes (this will be the tongue-and-groove joint that holds the frame together). Then lay each stile flat on the table saw table and use the miter gauge to feed the workpieces through the blade, trimming off the waste. Use a relief block clamped to the rip fence to line up the parts (See Photo C).

❺ Lay out the contour cuts in the bottoms of the lower rails, using the *Grid patterns* on page 70 as a reference. The peaks of the scalloped cutouts should be 1½ in. up from the bottom edge of each rail. For maximum accuracy, we made full-size templates for each of the cutout shapes and used them to trace the contours onto the workpieces (See Photo D). Cut out the scallops with a jig saw or a band saw and sand the contoured edges smooth.

❻ Cut the front, back and side panel inserts for the chest to size from ½-in. birch plywood. Fit the rails and stiles around the panel inserts to dry-assemble the chest panels, checking the fit as you go. The tenons at the ends of the stiles should fit snugly into the dado grooves in the inside edges of the rails. Once all four panels are dry-assembled, dry-fit the front, back and side panels together to check the carcase fit.

❼ Spread glue onto the tenons at the ends of the stiles and clamp the rails and stiles for each panel around the panel insert (See Photo E). Avoid getting glue into the grooves where the panel insert fits—the insert should float freely in the frame grooves. Check to make sure each glued-up panel is square by measuring the diagonals. Adjust the clamps until the lengths of the diagonal measurements are equal.

8 Cut the long, ½-in. × ½-in. tongues in the outside edges of the framed side panels. These tongues run the full, top-to-bottom length of each side. To make the tongues, we rabbeted both faces of the side-panel stiles with a dado-blade set **(See Photo F).**

9 Using the dado-blade set, cut a corresponding ½-in.-deep × ½-in.-wide dado along the edge of the inside face of both stiles on the front and back framed panels **(See Photo G).** The dadoes should start ¼ in. in from the outer edges. The tongues cut into the ends of the side panels should fit snugly into the dadoes in the front and back panels.
TIP: To ensure that your tongue-and-groove joints fit correctly, set up for the dado cuts, then make test cuts in 1-in.-thick scrap. Check the fit of the tongues into the scrap piece. Adjust the depth of the dado as needed before cutting the actual workpieces.

10 Chuck a ⅝-in. straight bit in your router and plow two ½-in.-deep dadoes along the inside faces of the front and back top rails **(See Photo H).** These grooves will serve as "tracks" for the ½-in.-thick sliding door panels. Locate the upper groove so the top shoulder is ½ in. down from the top edge of each rail, and cut a lower groove so the top shoulder is 1¾ in. down from the top edge (See *Detail,* page 70). Clamp a straightedge to the workpiece to guide the router. Be sure to stop the grooves at each end when they intersect the grooves made in the stiles. This way, the door tracks won't show when the carcase is assembled.

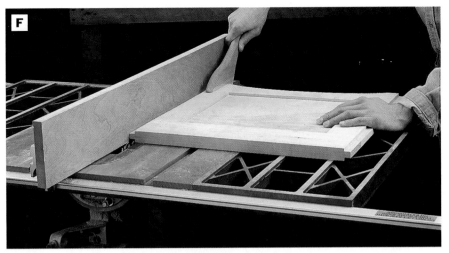

PHOTO F: Cut tongues into the outside edges of the stiles on the side frames, using a dado-blade set in the table saw. To protect your rip fence from the dado-blade set cutters, fit it with a sacrificial auxiliary fence made from scrapwood.

PHOTO G: Cut dadoes on the inside faces of the front and back panel frames to accept the tongues cut into the edges of the side panels.

PHOTO H: Cut stopped dadoes into the top rails of the front and back chest panel frames to serve as tracks for the sliding door panels. Guide the router against a straightedge, and stop the cuts at the points where they intersect the dadoes in the frame stiles.

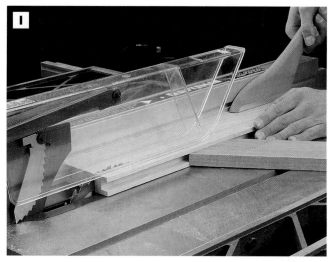

PHOTO I: Cut the grooves in the edges of the lid caps and ends before ripping the parts to finished width. A 1-in.-wide lid end is being cut to width in the photo above.

PHOTO J: Glue lid caps and ends to the lid panels, allowing ⅝ in. of panel to protrude along each side to serve as the lid runners.

MAKE THE CHEST LIDS

To minimize pinch points and add to the general safety of this toy chest, we designed the top with sliding lids that fit into grooves in the chest. The ends of the lids are fitted with 1-in.-thick poplar caps that hide the laminated edges of the plywood and help stiffen the lid panels.

⓫ Cut the two lid panels to size from ½-in. birch plywood.

⓬ Plane poplar stock for the lid caps and lid ends to a thickness of 1 in. The edges of the 2-in.-wide caps that join to the lids have ½-in.-wide × 1¼-in.-deep grooves that fit over the ends of the lids. One edge of both 1-in.-wide lid ends have ½-in.-wide × ½-in.-deep

grooves that fit over the ends of the lids. It's easiest (and safest) to cut the grooves before ripping the caps and ends to width. Use a dado-blade set on your table saw to cut a ½ × ½-in. groove in the edge of the stock, then rip-cut two end pieces to 1 in. wide (See Photo I). Using a featherboard and pushstick to hold the stock firmly against the fence and the table, cut a ½-in.-wide × 1¼-in.-deep dado in a long edge of the stock for each door cap. Make the dado in two passes—one with the dado set raised to ⅝ in. above the table, and then set to the full height of 1¼ in. Rip-cut the lid cap stock to 2 in. wide.

⓭ Cross-cut the lid ends and lid caps to 17¾ in. On each part, round the top and bottom of the long, flat edge (opposite the dadoed edge). Use a ¼-in. piloted roundover bit on the router table. Ease all remaining sharp edges and ends with sandpaper.

⓮ Select ¾-in. maple stock for the lid pulls. Make sure the board is at least 4 in. wide and the edges have been flattened and squared. *NOTE: Since the completed pulls are only ¾ in. wide and 1 in. tall, cutting them from wider stock keeps fingers a safe distance from cutters during the machining process.*

⓯ Round over the top and bottom of both long edges of the lid pulls on the router table using a ¼-in. roundover bit. Then rip the lid pulls to width on the table saw. Cross-cut the pulls to 15¾ in.

⓰ Glue and clamp the lid caps and ends to opposite edges of the lid panels (See Photo J). Each part should be centered on the end of the lid, leaving ⅝ in. of panel sticking out at each end to create runners that fit into the tracks in the upper chest rails.

ASSEMBLE THE CHEST

⓱ Dry assemble the chest to test the fit. Lay the carcase front down on its outside face on a work table and set the lids and sides into their respective tracks and grooves. Position the back of the carcase over the loose assembly and align the parts in the grooves.

⓲ Clamp the carcase across its width with bar or pipe clamps and wood cauls at each end. Set the chest right-side-up and test the operation of the lids in their tracks. Trim the door runners slightly to ensure their smooth operation in the tracks.

⓳ Dismantle the assembly. Spread glue evenly over all the tongues and grooves (but not the door tracks),

PHOTO K: Assemble the chest, fitting the lids into their grooves before gluing the tongue-and-groove joints at the corners.

PHOTO L: Attach the cleats that support the bottom panel to the inside faces of the lower chest rails, using screws driven into pilot holes.

PHOTO M: Prime and paint the toy chest. We painted the rails and stiles with white enamel paint, then painted each of the panels a different bright color.

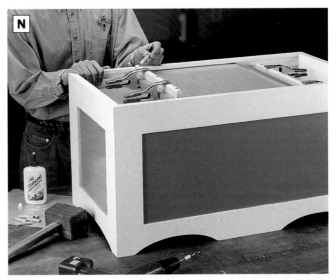

PHOTO N: Attach the maple lid pulls to the ends of the lids with ¼-in.-dia. dowels. Drill guide holes through the pulls and into the lid, then glue the pulls to the lid and drive in the dowels for reinforcement.

and fit the lids and sides into the fronts and backs **(See Photo K).** Clamp up the assembly, and check to make sure it's square by measuring the diagonals. Allow the glue to dry and remove the clamps.

⑳ Measure the inside bottom of the carcase, and cut the ½-in. plywood bottom panel to fit snugly.

㉑ Make up two 1 × 1 × 34-in. cleats and two 1 × 1 × 15¾-in. cleats from any scrap hardwood. Drill countersunk pilot holes at 8-in. intervals in one face of each cleat. Frame the inside of the chest with the cleats, positioning each one ¾ in. down from the top of the bottom rail it's attached to. Attach the cleats with 1-in. wallboard screws driven through the cleats and into the rails **(See Photo L).**

㉒ Slide the bottom panel inside the chest from below and attach it to the tops of the cleats with 1-in. wallboard screws driven into countersunk pilot holes. Cover the screw heads with wood putty.

APPLY FINISHING TOUCHES

㉓ Sand all the parts with 100-, then 120-grit sandpaper and ease all sharp edges and corners. Prime and paint the toy chest with child-safe enamel paint **(See Photo M).**

㉔ Attach the maple lid pulls to the lid caps with glue and ¼-in. dowels. **(See Photo N).** Trim the tops of the dowels flush with the top of the pull, then apply a protective finish to the pulls.

Mission Rocker

Truly a classic woodworking project, this handsome rocking chair features all the characteristics that make Mission furniture one of the most popular and enduring styles. Featuring the rich beauty of quartersawn oak, simple, elegant lines, and rock-solid pinned mortise-and-tenon joints, this rocker is an heirloom quality showpiece to be built and used with great pride.

Vital Statistics: Mission Rocker

TYPE: Rocking chair

OVERALL SIZE: 26W by 36H by 28D

MATERIAL: White oak

JOINERY: Pinned mortise-and-tenons, screw joints

CONSTRUCTION DETAILS:
- Rockers made from laminated strips of ¼-in. oak
- Tenoned back slats fit into mortises in rails
- Peak on crest rail for decorative touch
- Upholstered, padded seat

FINISHING OPTIONS: Medium to dark walnut stain with protective topcoat. Should have a darker, antique appearance.

Building time

PREPARING STOCK
3-4 hours

LAYOUT
3-4 hours

CUTTING PARTS
14-18 hours

ASSEMBLY
4-6 hours

FINISHING
4-6 hours

TOTAL: 28-38 hours

Tools you'll use

- Band saw
- Table saw
- Drill press
- Power miter saw
- Drill/driver
- Hand trim saw
- 40-in. or longer bar or pipe clamps (8)
- Wood mallet
- Wood chisel (¼-in.)
- File
- Power sander
- Combination square/ marking gauge
- Doweling jig
- Portable drill guide
- 2-in.-dia. hole saw
- Resawing guide
- Tenoning jig
- Stapler (electric or pneumatic)

Shopping list

- ☐ (1) 6/4 × 5½ in. × 8 ft. plain-sawn white oak
- ☐ (1) 6/4 × 3½ in. × 8 ft. plain-sawn white oak
- ☐ (2) ¾ × 6 in. × 8 ft. quartersawn white oak
- ☐ (1) ¾ × 4 in. × 8 ft. quartersawn white oak
- ☐ ¾-in. plywood scraps
- ☐ Finishing materials
- ☐ #10 × 2½-in. wood screws
- ☐ Wallboard screws (1¼, 2 in.)
- ☐ Upholstery fabric (36 × 36 in.)
- ☐ 4 × 16 × 19-in. foam
- ☐ ⅜-in.-dia. white oak plugs
- ☐ ¼-in.-dia. walnut doweling

Mission Rocker

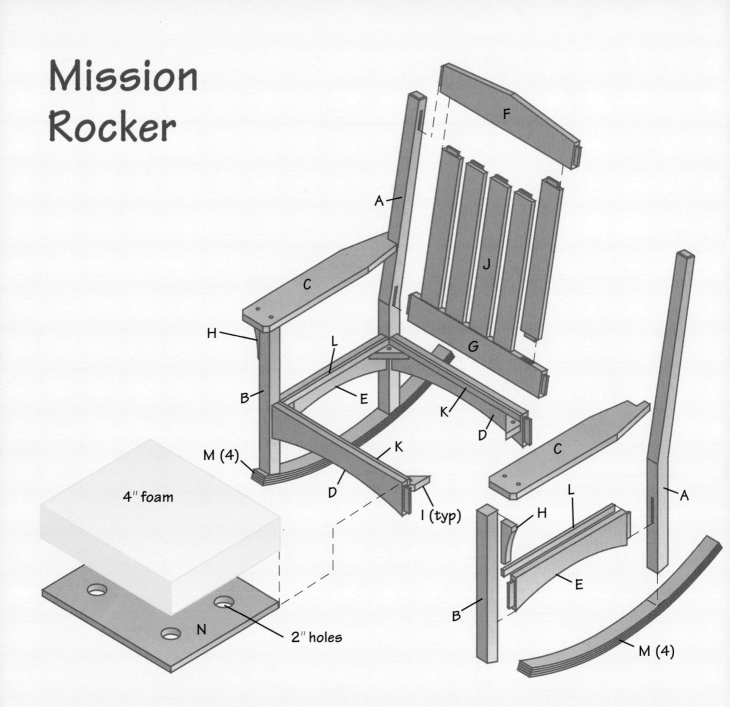

4″ foam

M (4)

2″ holes

I (typ)

Rocking Chair Cutting List

Part	No.	Size	Material	Part	No.	Size	Material
A. Back legs	2	1½ × 5½ × 36 in.	White oak	**H.** Corbels	2	¾ × 1½ × 5 in.	White oak (QS)
B. Front legs	2	1½ × 1½ × 19 in.	"	**I.** Corner blocks	4	¾ × 1½ × 4 in.	White oak
C. Arms	2	¾ × 4 × 21 in.	White oak (QS)	**J.** Back slats	5	½ × 2½ × 18 in.	White oak (QS)
D. Seat rails (front/back)	2	¾ × 4 × 20½ in.	"	**K.** Filler strips (front/back)	2	⅜ × ¾ × 19 in.	White oak
E. Seat rails (side)	2	¾ × 4 × 17½ in.	"	**L.** Filler strips (side)	2	⅜ × ¾ × 16 in.	"
F. Crest rail	1	¾ × 4 × 20 in.	"	**M.** Rocker plies	8	¼ × 2¼ × 32 in.	White oak (PS)
G. Lower back rail	1	¾ × 3 × 20½ in.	"	**N.** Seat board	1	¾ × 15⅝ × 18⅝ in.	Plywood

KEY: QS= quartersawn; PS= plain (face) sawn

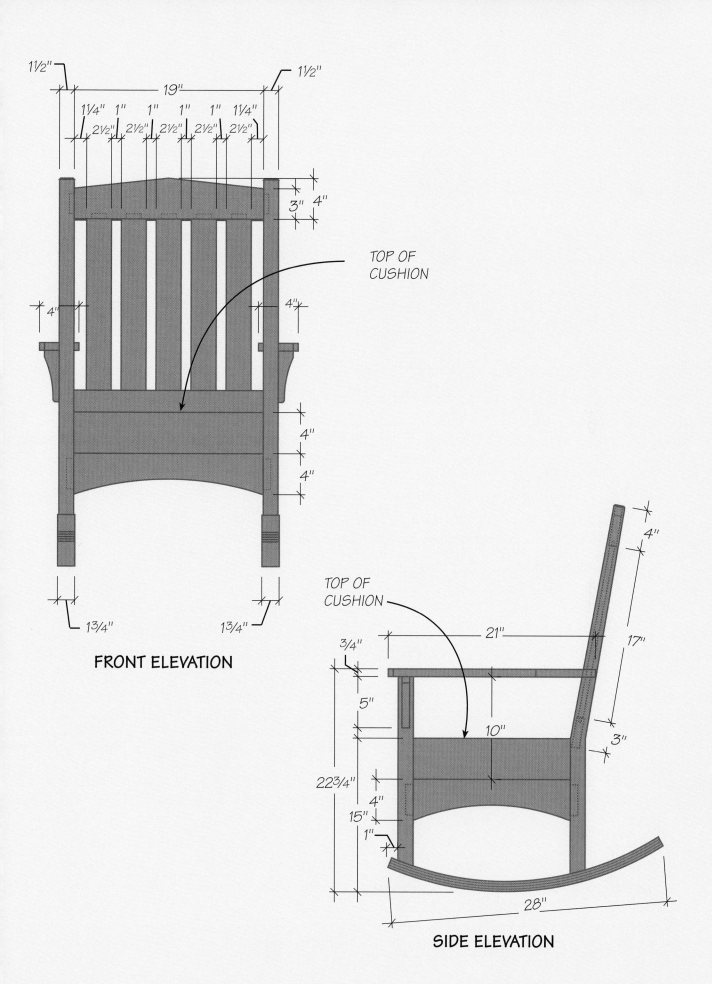

FRONT ELEVATION

SIDE ELEVATION

TOP OF CUSHION

TOP OF CUSHION

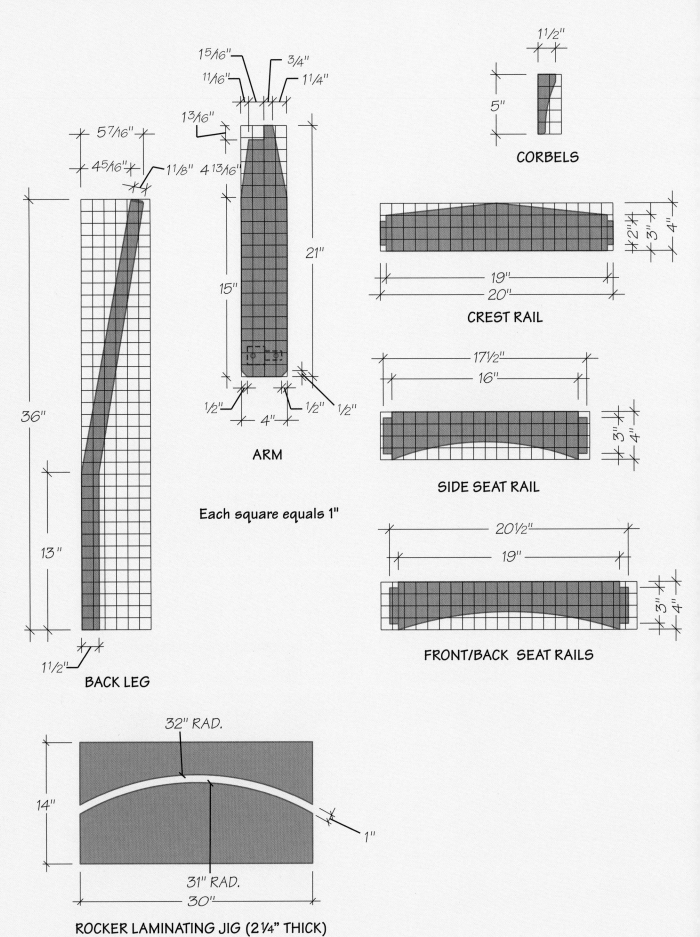

15/16"

3/4"

11/16"

1 1/4"

1 3/16"

1 1/2"

5"

CORBELS

5 7/16"

4 5/16"

1 1/8"

4 13/16"

21"

15"

36"

13"

2"

3"

4"

19"

20"

CREST RAIL

17 1/2"

16"

3"

4"

SIDE SEAT RAIL

1/2"

4"

1/2"

1/2"

ARM

Each square equals 1"

20 1/2"

19"

3"

4"

FRONT/BACK SEAT RAILS

1 1/2"

BACK LEG

32" RAD.

14"

1"

31" RAD.

30"

ROCKER LAMINATING JIG (2 1/4" THICK)

A NOTE: Blade guide raised to allow view of blade and jig. In practice, position the guide to within ¼ in. of workpiece.

Blade guide

PHOTO A: Use a band saw with a resawing guide to cut thin oak strips for the back slats and the lamination plies used to make the rockers.

PREPARE THE STOCK

In addition to routine squaring and planing of stock you'd do for any woodworking project, you'll need to resaw lumber into thin strips to build this rocker. You can purchase oak milled to ½ in. thick for the back slats and ¼ in. thick for the plies used to make the laminated rockers, but generally it's more economical to resaw thicker stock yourself. We used a band saw with a "pivot point" resawing jig to cut the thin strips.

❶ Select plain-sawn oak stock for resawing the ¼-in.-thick plies used to make the laminated rockers (using plain-sawn stock, where the grain runs parallel to the plies, allows it to conform to the curve of the rockers). Joint one edge of each board, then rip-cut to 2¼ in. wide and cross-cut to 32 in. long.

❷ Resaw the strips to ¼ in. thick, using a band saw and resawing jig (See *Tip,* right), or a table saw and rip fence. We used a ½-in.-wide, 4 tooth-per-inch, skip-tooth blade for the task. When resawing, cut the board slightly thicker than the finished width, since you'll need to plane it smooth after the cut is made. Lay the stock on the saw table with the jointed edge down, to ensure a square cut. Feed the stock into the blade, and angle the board as nec-

essary to keep it tight against the resawing guide **(See Photo A).** Feed the stock slowly enough that the blade isn't stressed, but not so slowly that it burns the wood. Cut enough stock to make all eight rocker plies, then plane the plies down to ¼ in. thick with your surface planer.

❸ Select stock for the ½-in.-thick back slats. We used quartersawn oak for the high-visibility parts of the chair, including the back slats. Due to the nature of the milling process, quartersawn lumber is most readily available in thinner dimensions. We chose ¾-in.-thick stock to make the back slats, removing ³⁄₁₆ in. by resawing, then planing the boards to ½ in. thick.

❹ Plane, joint and rip-cut stock for the rest of the chair parts, according to the thicknesses and widths listed in the *Cutting list* on page 78. Observe the notations made regarding grain pattern.

TIP **RESAWING GUIDE**

Clamping tail

Make a pivot-point resawing guide for resawing on the band saw. The guide should be slightly taller than the width of the stock you plan to resaw, and it should feature a tail for clamping. Taper the sides to a point in front (like the bow of a boat). Clamp the jig to the band saw table so the distance from the lead point to the blade is equal to the planned thickness of the resawn stock. Unlike a rip fence, this jig allows you to make adjustments while you feed the stock, counteracting the tendency of the thin blade to follow the grain pattern of the workpiece.

PHOTO B: Square off and clean up the mortises with a ¼-in. wood chisel. Use a drill press and ¼-in. brad-point bit or a router and ¼-in. straight bit to remove the wood in the mortise area.

Workpiece

Tenoning jig

PHOTO C: Cut the cheeks of the tenons on a table saw, using a tenoning jig that's sized so the horizontal member rides on top of the saw fence and the vertical member is flat on the table.

PHOTO D: After all cheek cuts are made, trim off the sides of the tenons, using the tenoning jig. Set the saw fence to remove ½ in. of wood from each side.

CUT & MACHINE THE PARTS

Because it's easier to cut tenons on square stock, do not make contour cuts on the seat rails and crest rails until after the tenons have been cut. As a general rule, cut the mortises first, then lay out and cut the tenons to fit.

5 Cut the 1½ × 5½ × 36-in.-long blanks for the back legs. Lay out the shapes of the legs on the blanks before cutting the rest of the chair parts to size—you should be able to cut several parts, including the front legs, from the waste areas left over after the back legs are cut. Use the *Grid pattern* on page 80 as a reference for plotting the back leg shape onto one of the blanks. Cut out the leg along the cutting lines, using a band saw or jig saw. Sand the back leg to its final shape and to smooth out any unevenness in the cut, then use the leg as a template for laying out the second back leg.

6 Cut out the second leg and the remaining chair parts, according to the dimensions given in the *Cutting list* on page 78. Sand the second leg to match the first.

7 Use a router with a chamfering bit, a stationary disc sander or a file to make four chamfers on the tops of the back legs.

8 Lay out and cut all the mortises in the legs and the crest rail and lower back rail. All mortises should be ¼ in. thick. Mortises for the back slats and the crest rail are ½ in. deep, and those for the tenons in the lower back rail and seat rails should be ¾ in. deep. The length of each mortise is 1 in. shorter than the width of the part it accepts (½ in. per side). Use a marking gauge to scribe the outline for each mortise, then remove the wood in the mortise area with a ¼-in.-dia. brad-point bit, or with a router and ¼-in. straight bit. Square off the ends and sides of each mortise with a sharp ¼-in. wood chisel **(See Photo B).**

❾ Lay out and cut the tenons in the ends of the seat slats, the crest rails, the lower back rail and the seat rails. Use a tenoning jig for your table saw to make the tenon cuts. Begin by making the ½- and ¾-in. deep cheek cuts **(See Photo C),** resetting the blade height and distance from the fence as needed. Then clamp the parts to the jig so the edges are against the fence and make cheek cuts for the sides of the tenons **(See Photo D).** Finish by cutting the tenon shoulders using your miter gauge to feed each piece through the blade. Clamp a relief block on the infeed side of the blade to set up the cuts **(See Photo E).** Test the fit of each tenon in the mating mortise, and trim the tenons with a chisel if they're too large.

❿ Lay out and cut the arches in the lower edges of the seat rails, using the *Grid patterns* on page 80 as references. Also lay out and cut the peak on the crest rail. The basic shape for the arms can be cut at this point also, although you'll need to transfer the angle of the back leg to bevel the front of the notch cut in the arms after the chair is assembled.

ASSEMBLE THE CHAIR

⓫ Finish-sand all exposed part surfaces and ease sharp edges. Don't sand tenons or any surfaces that will be joined together.

⓬ Dry-fit the parts for the back—the crest rail, the lower back rail,

PHOTO E: Cut the tenon shoulders, using a miter gauge to feed the workpieces over the blade. Clamp a relief block to the infeed side of the blade and use it to set up the cuts. Be sure to reset the blade height as needed to cut just up to each tenon.

PHOTO F: Assemble the back. Glue the back slats into the lower back rail first, then glue on the crest rail and clamp up the assembly, using clamp pads to protect the wood.

PHOTO G: Miter-cut the ends of the seat rail tenons so they'll meet to form clean miter joints inside the mortises in the legs. We used a sliding compound miter saw, but it could also be done on a table saw.

and the five slats. Then apply glue to the mortises and tenons and clamp up the assembly **(See Photo F).** Square-up the back by measuring the diagonals and adjusting the clamps as necessary.

⓭ The tenons of the seat rails are designed to meet inside the mortises in the legs. Cut a 45° miter

at the ends of each tenon so they'll fit together neatly inside the legs. We used a power miter saw to make the miter cuts **(See Photo G).**

⓮ Glue and clamp the back assembly and the back seat rail into their joints between the two back legs. Also glue up the front

PHOTO H: Glue up the chair in stages to keep control of the work. Here, the front seat rail is attached between the front legs.

PHOTO I: Glue the side rails into the back legs, then attach the front assembly to the side rails. Clamp up the whole framework, checking the diagonals to make sure it's square.

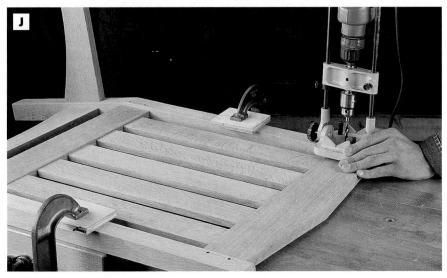

PHOTO J: Drill guide holes for the ¼-in. dowels used to pin the mortise-and-tenon joints. A portable drill guide ensures perpendicular holes drilled to the correct depth.

seat rail to the front legs and clamp (See Photo H).

⑮ Now glue and clamp the front assembly to the back, with the side seat rails between them (See Photo I). Check to make sure all parts are square to one another and adjust the clamping pressure, if needed, before the glue sets.

⑯ Lay out and drill holes for the ¼-in.-dia. dowels used to pin the tenons that fit into the front and back legs. We used walnut doweling for a dramatic, contrasting appearance. Use two pins for each joint, taking care to align the dowel guide holes. We used a portable drill guide to ensure that the dowel holes are perpendicular and deep enough to extend all the way through the tenon and into the wood on the opposite side of each mortise (See Photo J). Beyond their ornamental aspect, these also serve to lock the tenon joints. Apply glue to the end of each pin and drive it home with a wood mallet. Trim the top of the pin flush after the glue cures.

⑰ Glue and clamp the four seat filler strips to the insides of the seat rails. Their top edges should be flush with the top edges of the rails. The filler strips create a square opening for the seat board.

⑱ Drill a countersunk screw hole through the underside of each corner block, to be used to screw the seat down. Drill countersunk screw holes to attach the corner blocks to the seat rails, just below the filler strips. Glue and screw them in place with 1¼-in. wall-board screws (See Photo K).

ATTACH THE ARMS
⑲ Glue and clamp the corbels to the front legs. They should be cen-

PHOTO K: Apply glue, then screw the corner blocks in place just below the filler strips, using 1¼-in. wallboard screws.

PHOTO L: With the arm level and resting on the front leg, trace the angle of the back leg creating a bevel line to cut the arm notch.

PHOTO M: Glue and screw the arms to the chair frame. Drive two screws into the leg/corbel support and one into the back leg.

tered on the legs and flush with the leg tops.

⓴ Lay each arm in place, resting on the front leg and corbel. Keeping the arm level, hold the back end against the back leg. Mark the angle of the back leg onto the edge of each arm, starting at the end of the notch at the top **(See Photo L).** Remove the arms and use a small hand trim or back saw to bevel the notches along the cutting line.

㉑ Fit the arms in place and center them on the front leg/corbel assembly. Drill and counterbore screw holes so the screws can be plugged, then screw the arms down with two 2-in. wallboard screws each **(See Photo M).** Drive one screw to attach each arm to its back leg.

㉒ Plug the screw holes with ⅜-in.-dia. white oak plugs and sand the plugs flush.

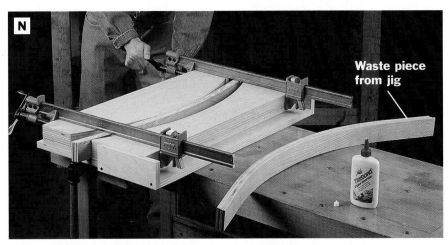

PHOTO N: Press the oak plies together in a laminating jig to face-glue the blanks for the rockers. The plywood base and the short sides help keep the two halves of the jig aligned during the glue up. Let the glue dry overnight before removing each glued-up rocker blank.

MAKE THE ROCKERS

㉓ Make the bending jig (See *Rocker jig illustration,* page 80) from three layers of scrap plywood or particleboard, glued up to make a 2¼ × 14 × 30-in. blank.

㉔ Draw the two different radius curves 1 in. apart on the blank, and cut them out with a band saw. Cut a 30-in.-sq. piece of plywood

for a jig base and screw ½ of the jig form to it. Attach short strips of plywood to the edges of the base at the top of the jig (these will help keep the moveable half of the jig aligned with the fixed half when the rocker plies are clamped between them). Wax the curved surfaces of the jig to keep the glue from sticking.

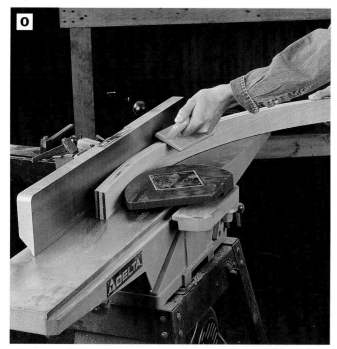

PHOTO O: After laminating, joint one edge of each rocker flat and square. Keep the outer face against the fence and carefully feed the rocker along its curve, using push blocks to guide the workpiece.

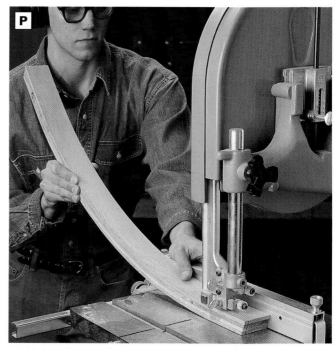

PHOTO P: Use the rip fence of your band saw as a guide to rip-cut the rockers to 1¾ in. wide. Keep the jointed edge against the fence. If you don't have a rip fence, clamp a straightedge to the table.

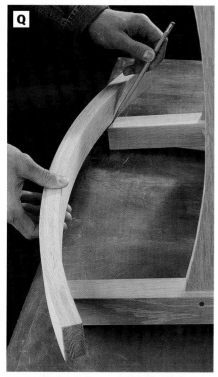

PHOTO Q: Scribe the arc of the rockers onto the leg bottoms by holding the rockers in proper position against the legs and marking with a pencil. Trim the bottoms of the legs to follow the curved cutting lines, using a hand saw to remove most of the wood. Smooth out the cuts with a sander or file.

PHOTO R: Attach the rockers to the legs with glue and one #10 × 2½-in. wood screw driven through a counterbored pilot hole. Plug the counterbores with ⅜-in.-dia. wood plugs.

㉕ Spread glue on the mating surfaces of four of the ¼-in.-thick plies and stack them together face to face.

㉖ Position the glued-up plies between the two halves of the laminating jig and begin tightening clamps at each end, adjusting the glue-up to keep it centered in the jig and to keep the edges of the plies aligned (See Photo N). Tighten the clamps a little at a time, alternating between ends, until the plies are pressed together tightly. Add another clamp in the middle.

㉗ Leave the rocker in the jig overnight. Then remove it and glue up the other rocker.

㉘ Scrape as much of the dried glue as you can from one edge of each rocker with a paint scraper. Then clean up and square the edge by flattening it on a jointer, keeping the outer face of the glue-up against the fence (See Photo O).

㉙ Rip-cut the rockers to 1¾ in. wide, using a band saw with a rip fence (See Photo P).

㉚ Cut the ends of the rockers square to the curve. You can square a line and cut the ends on a band saw or make the cuts on a table saw, chop saw, or with a back saw in a miter box. The finished length of the rockers should be 28 in., measured in a straight line from end to end.

㉛ Hold each rocker in place against the front and back legs and scribe the line of the curve on the bottoms of the legs. Start the curves at the inside, bottom edges of the legs (See Photo Q). Use a hand saw to remove the waste, then smooth out the cuts with a file or sander.

㉜ Finish-sand the rockers. Lay the chair upside down on its arms and rest the rockers on the leg bottoms. Center the legs on the rockers, and adjust the rockers so their front ends protrude 1 in. in front of the front legs. Drill countersunk pilot holes, then attach the rockers with glue and one #10 × 2½-in. screw per leg (See Photo R). Plug the counterbores with white oak plugs.

FINISHING TOUCHES

㉝ Touch up any rough areas with sandpaper. Apply your desired finish. We used walnut-tinted Danish oil with a tung oil topcoat.

㉞ Cut the seat board to size from scrap ¾-in. plywood. Use a hole saw to drill four 2-in.-dia. vent holes in the seat board.

㉟ Cut a piece of 4-in.-thick high-density foam the same dimensions as the seat board, then center the foam on the underside of a 36-in.-sq. piece of upholstery fabric. Neatly tuck the upholstery around the corners and tack it to the bottom of the seat board with a pneumatic stapler or upholstery tacks (See Photo S). You may want to hire an upholsterer to make the seat, especially if you cover it with leather.

㊱ Attach the upholstered seat with 1¼-in. wallboard screws driven up through the pilot holes in the corner blocks (See Photo T).

PHOTO S: You can upholster the chair seat yourself by using a pneumatic or electric stapler to tack a 36-in.-sq. piece of upholstery fabric over 4-in. foam. Work carefully when making the corners.

Dust-block fabric

PHOTO T: Attach the seat with screws driven up through the corner blocks and into the seat board.

Formal Bookcase

Built with walnut-veneer plywood and a solid walnut face frame, this bookcase has a rich, formal appearance. The design is highlighted by walnut shelf-edge trim with an ogee profile. Decorative appliques accent the contours of the top face frame rail. This is a simple project with fine-furniture appeal.

Vital Statistics: Formal Bookcase

TYPE: Bookcase

OVERALL SIZE: 31½W by 60¾H by 10¾D

MATERIAL: Walnut and walnut plywood

JOINERY: Rabbet and dado joints, dowel joints in face frame

CONSTRUCTION DETAILS:
- Fixed center shelf fits into stopped dadoes in standards
- Three adjustable shelves
- Shelf-edge is profiled with ogee router bit
- Decorative birch appliques treated with walnut stain

FINISHING OPTIONS: Clear coat with tung oil varnish. For more even color, apply light walnut stain to darken plywood.

Building time

PREPARING STOCK
1 hour

LAYOUT
1-2 hours

CUTTING PARTS
3-5 hours

ASSEMBLY
2-4 hours

FINISHING
1-2 hours

TOTAL: 8-14 hours

Tools you'll use

- Circular saw with plywood cutting blade
- Straightedge cutting guide
- C-clamps
- Router table with piloted ¾-in. ogee bit
- Router with ¾-in. straight bit and ⅜-in. rabbet bit
- Tape measure
- 36-in. or longer bar or pipe clamps (6)
- Jig saw, band saw or scroll saw
- Hammer and tack hammer
- Combination square
- Doweling jig
- Drill/driver
- Nailset
- Stopped dado jig (See page 92)
- Pegboard drilling guide (See page 94)

Shopping list

- ☐ (1) ¾ × 4 ft. × 8 ft. sheet veneer-core walnut plywood
- ☐ (1) ¼ × 4 ft. × 8 ft. sheet plywood (walnut or other) for back panel
- ☐ (1) ¾ × 4 in. × 8 ft. walnut for face frame and shelf-edge strips
- ☐ Decorative appliques for top rail
- ☐ (1) ⅜-in.-dia. wood dowel for shelf pins
- ☐ Finishing materials
- ☐ 1-in. wire brads, 4d finish nails
- ☐ Wood glue

Formal Bookcase

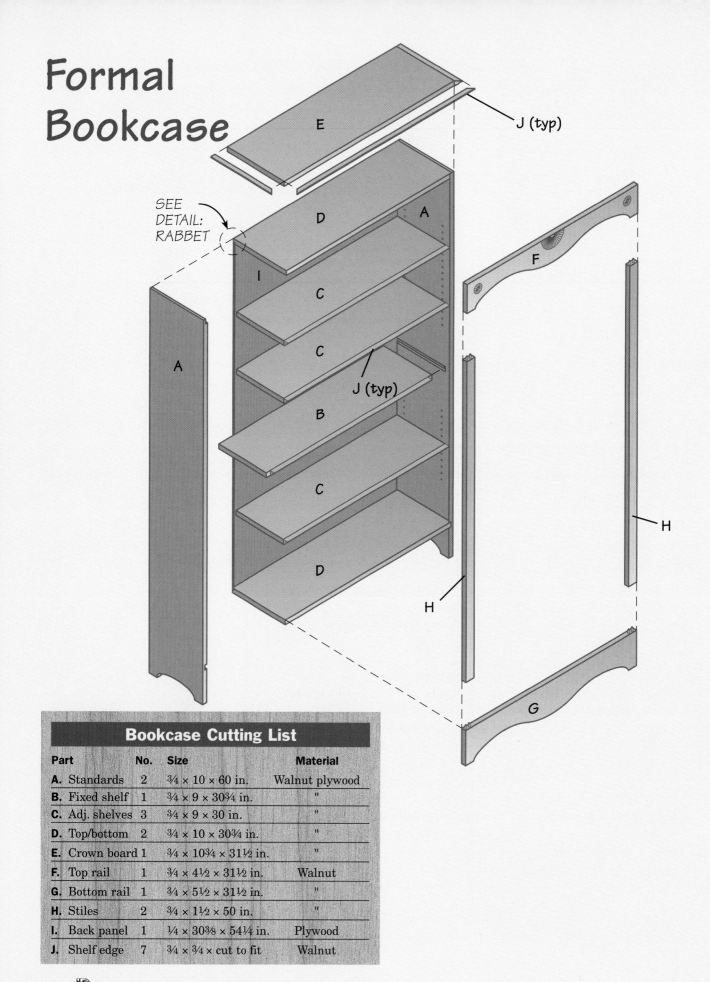

J (typ)

E

SEE DETAIL: RABBET

D   A

I

C

C

A

J (typ)

B

C

D

F

H

H

G

H

Bookcase Cutting List

Part	No.	Size	Material
A. Standards	2	¾ × 10 × 60 in.	Walnut plywood
B. Fixed shelf	1	¾ × 9 × 30¾ in.	"
C. Adj. shelves	3	¾ × 9 × 30 in.	"
D. Top/bottom	2	¾ × 10 × 30¾ in.	"
E. Crown board	1	¾ × 10¾ × 31½ in.	"
F. Top rail	1	¾ × 4½ × 31½ in.	Walnut
G. Bottom rail	1	¾ × 5½ × 31½ in.	"
H. Stiles	2	¾ × 1½ × 50 in.	"
I. Back panel	1	¼ × 30⅜ × 54¼ in.	Plywood
J. Shelf edge	7	¾ × ¾ × cut to fit	Walnut

Each square equals 1"

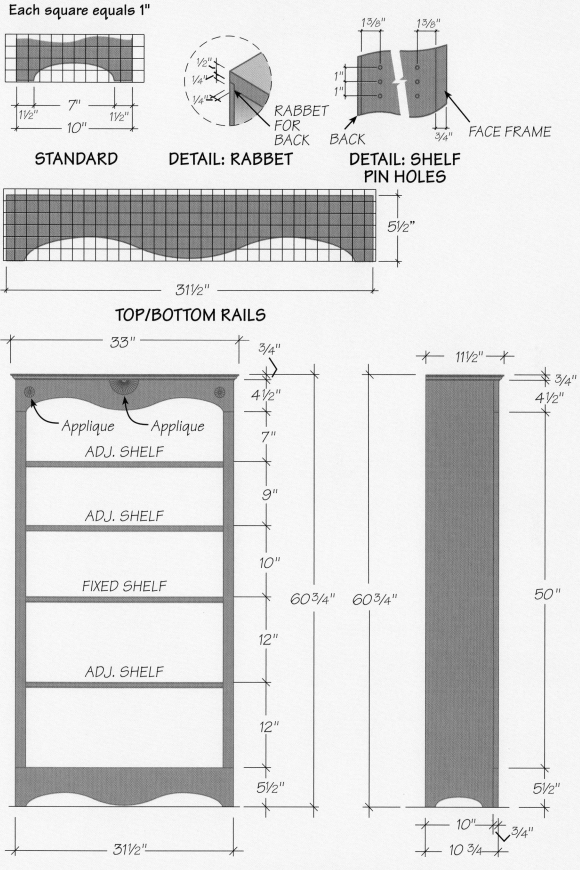

STANDARD

DETAIL: RABBET

¹/₂"
¹/₄"
¹/₄"

RABBET FOR BACK

1³/₈"   1³/₈"

1"
1"

BACK

³/₄"

FACE FRAME

DETAIL: SHELF PIN HOLES

5¹/₂"

31¹/₂"

TOP/BOTTOM RAILS

33"

³/₄"

Applique   Applique

ADJ. SHELF

4¹/₂"

7"

ADJ. SHELF

9"

FIXED SHELF

10"

60³/₄"

ADJ. SHELF

12"

12"

5¹/₂"

31¹/₂"

11¹/₂"

³/₄"

4¹/₂"

60³/₄"

50"

5¹/₂"

10"
10 ³/₄

³/₄"

ELEVATIONS (SIDE & FRONT)

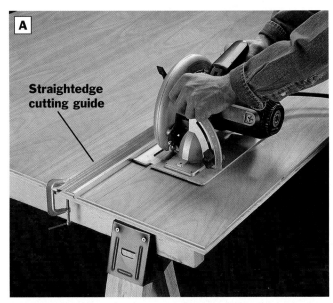

PHOTO A: Cut the plywood parts using a circular saw and straightedge cutting guide. The plywood should be good-face-down.

Straightedge cutting guide

PHOTO B: Profile the jointed edge of a strip of walnut, using an ogee bit mounted in your router table. Rip the profiled edge to ¾ in. wide.

PHOTO C: Make a jig for cutting the stopped dadoes in the standards. An L-shaped jig like the one above provides a straight edge for the router base to follow and also creates a stopping point.

CUT THE PLYWOOD PARTS

All the plywood parts for this bookcase (except the ¼-in.-thick back panel) are cut from a single piece of ¾-in. plywood. Because we wanted to achieve a rich, formal appearance, we used walnut-veneer plywood and trimmed it with a solid walnut face frame. Walnut plywood is available at most lumberyards (you likely won't find it at a general building center), but it is among the most expensive plywood types. For economy, you could use oak plywood with oak trim and still end up with a very attractive bookcase. Whichever type of plywood you use, make sure the sheet you purchase is created with cabinet-grade veneer on both faces. *Tip: For economy, sketch a cutting diagram before you start cutting the parts.*

① Begin by rip-cutting two 9-in.-wide strips from the plywood sheet to make the fixed shelf and the three adjustable shelves **(See Photo A).** Rip-cut 10 in.-wide-strips for the top, the bottom and the two standards (the bookcase sides). Cut the crown board to 10¾ in. wide. Then cross-cut all parts to length according to the *Cutting list* (page 90).

MAKE THE SHELVES

We used strips of shelf-edge trim to conceal the edges of the plywood shelves. The shelf-edge is made by profiling walnut boards on a router table, then ripping them to width. If you prefer, you can simply rip-cut ¾-in.-wide strips of solid wood and round over or chamfer the edges. If you're building your bookcase with oak or pine, you may be able to find premilled shelf-edge at a lumberyard.

② Mount a piloted profiling bit with a ½-in. shank into your router table—we used a ¾-in. ogee bit. Joint one edge of a ¾-in.-thick walnut board, then pass the jointed edge over the router bit to create the profile **(See Photo B).** Rip-cut a ¾-in.-wide strip from the profiled edge of the board, using a table saw. Continue profiling and ripping edge strips until you have enough shelf-edge for all the shelves and for the front and sides of the crown board (about 16 lineal ft.).

❸ Cut four strips of shelf-edge to 30 in. long for the shelves (the shelf-edge is inset ⅜ in. from each end of the fixed shelf). Attach the shelf-edge with glue and 1 in. wire nails driven through pilot holes at 8- to 10-in. intervals. Do not attach the shelf-edge for the crown board yet.

MAKE THE STANDARDS

❹ Transfer the *Grid pattern* (page 91) for the cutouts on the bottoms of the standards to the standard workpieces. *Tip: Use a white colored pencil to draw cutting lines on dark wood like walnut.* Use a band saw, jig saw or scroll saw to cut out the shape (for uniform results, gang the standards together). Cut just to the waste side of each line. Use a rasp, file or sandpaper wrapped around a dowel to smooth the contours.

❺ Cut a ¾-in.-wide × ⅜-in.-deep stopped dado in each standard for the fixed shelf. The tops of the dadoes should be 29½ in. up from the bottom of each standard. Stop the dadoes ¾ in. from the front edge of each standard and square them off with a chisel **(See Photo C).** Cutting stopped dadoes with a router and straight bit requires a stopblock. We made an L-shaped jig that is clamped to the workpiece, as seen in **Photo C**. The jig is sized for the setback distance of the router bit from the edge of the router foot. When positioned properly, it ensures that the router follows a straight cutting line, as well as provides a stopping point for the cut. Make the cuts in at least two passes, increasing the cutting depth with each pass.

❻ With your router and straight bit (or on a table saw), cut a ¾-in.-wide × ⅜-in.-deep dado on the inside face of each standard for the bottom of the bookcase. Locate the top of each dado 5½ in. up from the bottom of each standard.

❼ Cut a ¾-in.-wide × ⅜-in.-deep rabbet at the top of each standard to accept the top.

ASSEMBLE THE CARCASE

❽ Dry-assemble the bookcase carcase, with the top, bottom, and fixed shelf in place. This is an important step that allows you to make any adjustments necessary in the joints so the fit is right. It also is your

PHOTO D: Measure the diagonals between corners of the carcase to check for square. Adjust the clamps until the diagonals are equal.

PHOTO E: Cut a ¼ × ¼-in. rabbet groove all the way around the back inside edge of the carcase to provide a recess for the back panel. Square off the cuts at the corners with a chisel.

opportunity to make sure your planned clamping technique will work. As you disassemble the setup, keep the clamps at the same settings and close at hand. Lay out the parts and spread glue evenly into the dadoes and rabbets. Clamp the carcase up, using ¾ in. cauls to protect the wood and spread the clamping pressure across the sides. After all the clamps are on, measure the diagonals of the bookcase to see if it's square **(See Photo D).** Adjust the carcase by shifting the clamps until the diagonal measurements are equal. Remove glue squeeze-out with an old chisel after a film has formed on the glue. Leave the clamps on until the glue is cured.

❾ Lay the bookcase down on its front edge and rabbet the back inside edge of the carcase to accept the back **(See Photo E).** Use a router with a piloted

PHOTO F: Tack profiled shelf-edge around the front and sides of the crown board, mitering the corners.

PHOTO G: Cut the decorative contours in the top and bottom face frame rails on your band saw, or with a jig saw.

¼-in. rabbet bit to rout a ¼- × ¼-in. rabbet all the way around. Rest the router base on the back edge of the carcase and carefully hold the router straight and plumb as you run it along with the pilot bearing riding against the inside of the plywood. The bearing will stop in the corners, leaving a rounded, partially cut rabbet. You'll need to square off the corners of the rabbet with a chisel, as well as finish the rabbet cut next to the fixed shelf (the shelf will obstruct the router bit as you make the rabbet cut).

⑩ Measure the overall dimensions of the rabbeted opening and cut the ¼ in.-plywood back panel to fit. If you're using non-walnut plywood (cheaper maple plywood is shown here), stain the front face to match the walnut plywood. When the stain is dry, install the panel using 1-in. wire brads—no glue. Nail carefully into the rabbet, angling the brads toward the outside so they don't break through the inside face of the carcase. Mark a line on the back panel, centered over the fixed shelf. Drive brads through the back and into the fixed shelf along the line.

⑪ Drill holes for the adjustable shelf pins. A drilling guide made from perforated tempered hardboard (pegboard) makes drilling evenly spaced holes easy. Cut a strip of pegboard to fit into the top and bottom sides of the bookcase. Rip one edge so it's 1⅜ in. from the centerline of a row of holes. Measure 6 in. up from the bottom and 6 in. down from the top and start marking drilling points through the holes in the pegboard. Drill your holes using a depth marker

(like masking tape) set to ⅜ in. on your drill bit. Keep the drill as close to perpendicular as you can.

ATTACH THE CROWN BOARD

⑫ Test the fit of the crown board, then attach it to the top of the bookcase carcase with glue and 4d finish nails. It should be flush with the outside and back edges of the carcase and overhang the front by ¾ in. Miter-cut three pieces of shelf-edge to frame the crown board and attach them with glue and 4d finish nails **(See Photo F)**.

MAKE & ATTACH THE FACE FRAME

⑬ Rip two strips of ¾-in. walnut to 1½ in. wide × 50 in. long for the face frame stiles. Cut a 4½- × 31½-in. top rail and a 5½- × 31½-in. bottom rail (be sure to check your measurements against the actual size of the bookcase for an accurate fit).

⑭ Transfer the contour shown in the *Grid pattern* on page 91 onto the top rail, starting 1½ in. in from each end. Cut the profile using a band saw or jig saw and sand or file the edges smooth **(See Photo G)**.

⑮ Using the top rail as a template, draw the contour onto the bottom rail. Cut out the shape on the bottom rail and sand the profile smooth.

⑯ The face frame should be assembled separately, then attached to the carcase. We used dowels to reinforce the butt joints at the corners of the face frame. Biscuits, splines, pocket screws or even finish nails

PHOTO H: Reinforce the corner joints on the face frame. We used a doweling jig to make dowel joints.

PHOTO I: Set all exposed nail heads with a nailset, then fill the nail holes with walnut-tinted wood putty. Sand all wood surfaces with 150-then 180-grit sandpaper.

could be used instead. To make the dowel joints, use a doweling jig and drill two dowel holes in each joint between the rails and stiles (**See Photo H**). Assemble the face frame using glue and clamps. Check with a framing square or by measuring the diagonals to make sure the face frame is square.

17 Attach the face frame to the bookcase carcase with glue and 4d finish nails. Be sure to drill pilot holes before nailing to avoid splitting the wood. You can use a small drill bit, or just cut off the head of one of the finish nails and chuck it in the drill. Sink the nails with a nailset (**See Photo I**).

APPLY FINISHING TOUCHES

Decorative wood appliques on the top rail add interest and give this bookcase a more formal appearance. You can buy unfinished wood appliques at most woodworking stores or craft stores, and from woodworking supply catalogs. The birch appliques we used are stock numbers WC3040 and WC3001 from *Constantine's Woodworker's Catalog.*

18 Stain the appliques to match the color of the face frame material—we used a light walnut stain. After the stain dries, lay the appliques on the top rail and adjust them until you're satisfied with their location. Make small reference marks around the appliques with a white pencil or with pieces of tape (**See Photo J**). Glue them in place using your marks to guide you in positioning, and secure them with padded clamps or a heavy object until the glue dries.

PHOTO J: Use tape or a white pencil to mark reference lines for the appliques, then glue the appliques to the top rail.

19 Fill all nail holes with walnut-tinted wood putty. Finish-sand all surfaces, including the adjustable shelves, with 150-grit sandpaper, then 180-grit. Wipe the surfaces with a tack cloth. Apply the finish of your choice to all parts according to the manufacturer's directions. We mixed our own blend of ⅓ turpentine, ⅓ linseed oil, and ⅓ varnish and applied three coats.

20 Insert shelf pins (either brass or wood dowels) into the shelf pin holes at the desired heights and install the adjustable shelves.

Porch Swing

A cool breeze and a calming motion are the main returns you'll earn if you invest a little time and money in building this porch swing. Made of lightweight cedar (or any exterior wood), this swing will seat two adults comfortably while standing up to any abuse the elements can send its way.

Vital Statistics: Porch Swing

TYPE: Two-person outdoor swing

OVERALL SIZE: 58½W by 26H by 30D

MATERIAL: Cedar

JOINERY: Half-lap joints reinforced with glue and screws, butt joints reinforced with screws

CONSTRUCTION DETAILS:
· All parts cut from standard dimensional cedar
· Comfortable slope to seat and back rest
· Four eyebolts for hanging
· Three slat supports distribute weight evenly

FINISHING OPTIONS: Clear coat with UV-resistant wood sealer, stain with exterior stain or paint white or gray for a more formal appearance.

Building time

PREPARING STOCK
1 hour

LAYOUT
2-4 hours

CUTTING PARTS
3-5 hours

ASSEMBLY
2-4 hours

FINISHING
1-2 hours

TOTAL: 9-16 hours

Tools you'll use

· Table saw
· Band saw or jig saw
· Drill press
· C-clamps
· Router table with piloted ¼-in. roundover bit
· Tape measure
· Spring clamps
· Drill/driver
· Portable drill guide
· Dado-blade set for table saw

Shopping list

☐ (5) 2 × 6 in. × 8 ft. (nominal) cedar

☐ (4) 1 × 6 in. × 8 ft. (nominal) cedar

☐ (4) ⅜ × 4-in. eyebolts; ⅜-in. nuts and washers

☐ Galvanized deck screws (2-, 2½-, 3-in.)

☐ Finishing materials

☐ 30-40 ft. heavy rope (not cotton) or chain

☐ Weatherproof wood glue

Porch Swing

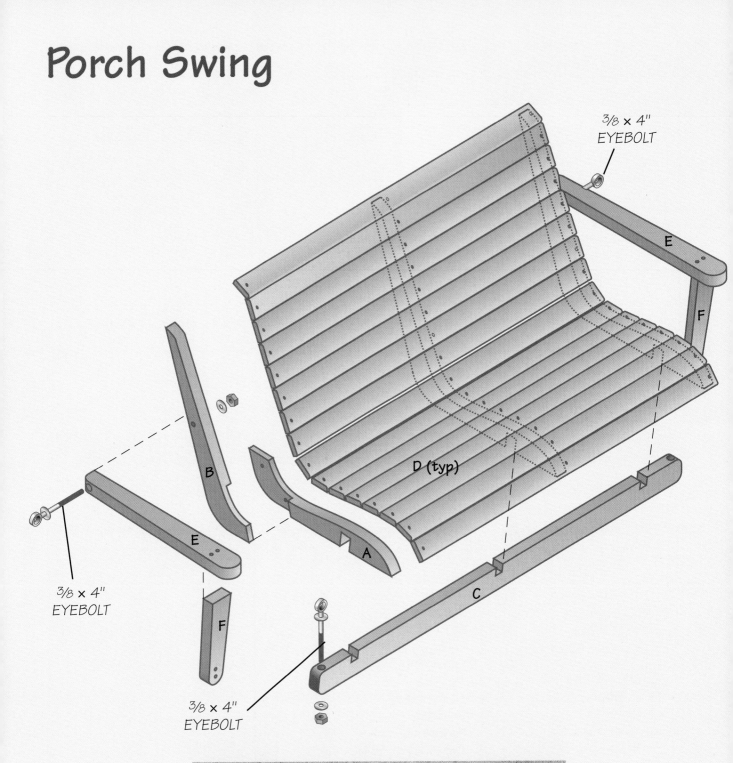

3/8 × 4"
EYEBOLT

E

F

D (typ)

B

A

C

3/8 × 4"
EYEBOLT

E

F

3/8 × 4"
EYEBOLT

Porch Swing Cutting List

Part	No.	Size	Material
A. Seat supports	3	1½ × 5¼* × 24 in.	Cedar
B. Back supports	3	1½ × 5¼* × 25½ in.	"
C. Cross support	1	1½ × 3 × 58½ in.	"
D. Slats	16	¾ × 2½ × 48 in.	"
E. Arms	2	1½ × 3 × 25 in.	"
F. Arm supports	2	1½ × 3 × 13 in.	"

* Width of rough stock prior to finished cutting

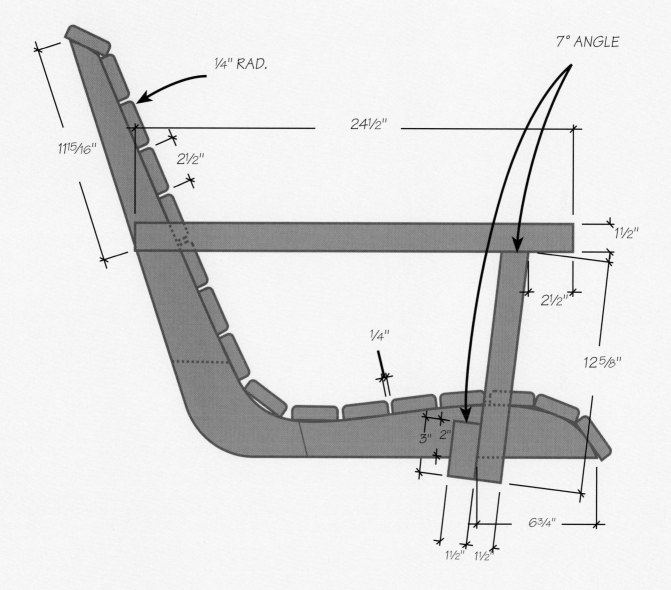

7° ANGLE

¼" RAD.

24½"

11¹⁵⁄₁₆"

2½"

1½"

2½"

12⅝"

¼"

3" 2"

6¾"

1½" 1½"

SIDE ELEVATION

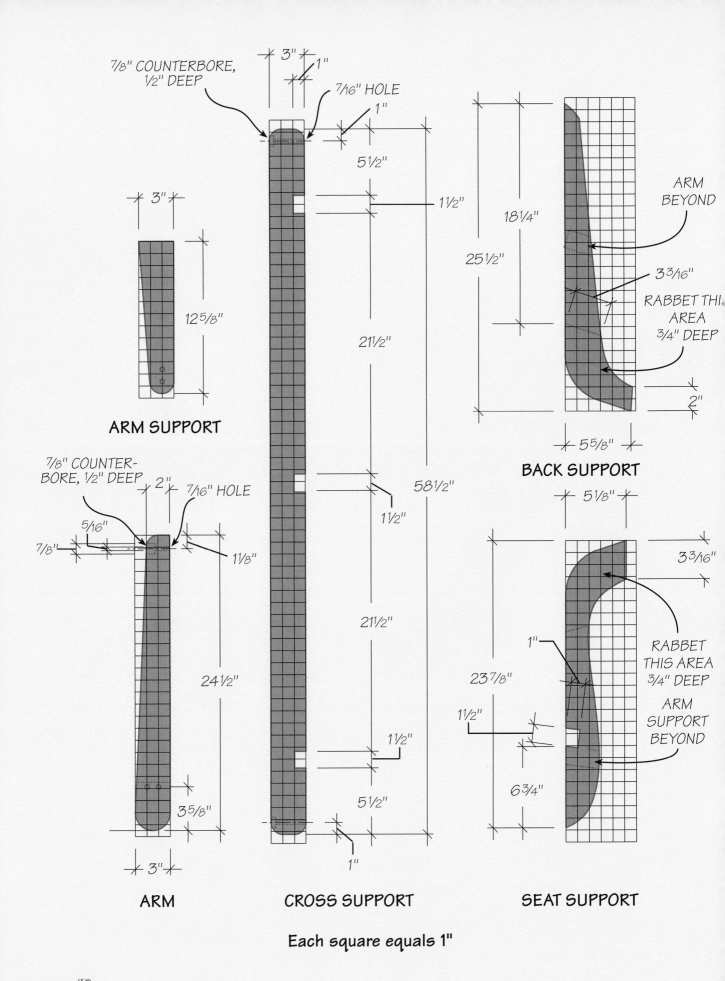

ARM SUPPORT

ARM

CROSS SUPPORT

BACK SUPPORT

SEAT SUPPORT

Each square equals 1"

7/8" COUNTERBORE, 1/2" DEEP

3"

1"

7/16" HOLE

1"

5 1/2"

1 1/2"

3"

12 5/8"

21 1/2"

58 1/2"

1 1/2"

21 1/2"

1 1/2"

5 1/2"

1"

7/8" COUNTER-BORE, 1/2" DEEP

2"

7/16" HOLE

5/16"

7/8"

1 1/8"

24 1/2"

3 5/8"

3"

18 1/4"

25 1/2"

ARM BEYOND

3 3/16"

RABBET THI AREA 3/4" DEEP

2"

5 5/8"

5 1/8"

3 3/16"

1"

RABBET THIS AREA 3/4" DEEP

ARM SUPPORT BEYOND

23 7/8"

1 1/2"

6 3/4"

Porch Swing: Step-by-step

MAKE THE SUPPORT ASSEMBLY
The structural members of this porch swing consist of three L-shaped, two-part supports that are fitted over a thick horizontal cross support in front. To simplify the layout and construction of the two-part supports, we joined the parts together with half-lap joints before any of the contoured profiles were cut.

1 Start by making a full-size template of the back support and seat supports shapes, using the *Grid patterns* on page 100 as references. Either enlarge the patterns on a photocopier or draw a grid on the template paper and plot out the shapes.

2 Cut 2 × 6 cedar blanks for the seat supports and back supports to the lengths listed in the *Cutting list* on page 98. Lay the blanks next to one another in pairs, in an "L" shape, on a flat surface. Overlap the seat support and back support templates so they join together at the half-lap joint lines indicated on the pattern. Lay the templates onto each pair of 2 × 6 blanks and mark the positions of the half-lap cuts onto the blanks.

3 Cut the half-laps into the 2 × 6 blanks. Install a dado-blade set, set for its maximum cutting

PHOTO A: Cut the half-laps in the seat supports and back supports with a dado-blade set, making multiple overlapping passes. The final pass on each board should be right along the marked cutting line. Set the miter gauge to 65°. Making the half-lap joints prior to cutting the contours of the parts simplifies the layout of the contours.

PHOTO B: Set the cutting angle of the dado-blade set to 7° and cut 1-in.-deep notches for the seat supports into the bottom edges of the seat supports.

PHOTO C: Glue and clamp the half-laps of the seat supports and the back supports together to create L-shaped blanks for the three support structures. Use weatherproof glue.

PHOTO D: Use a template to transfer the patterns of the back supports and seat supports onto the glued-up blanks, and cut out the shapes with a band saw or jig saw.

width, in the table saw. Raise the dado-blade set to a ¾-in. cutting depth. Set the angle of the miter gauge to 65° (the angle of the half-laps). Keeping the wood pressed flat on the table and held firmly against the miter gauge fence, run the appropriate end of each blank over the dado blades to remove the wood in the half-lap area **(See Photo A).** Make multiple passes. The final pass should be right to the cutting line. Cut the half-laps in all three pairs of blanks.

❹ Use the same dado set to cut notches in the bottoms of the seat supports. Angle the blades to 7°, and reset the miter gauge to 90°. Raise the blades to give a 1-in. depth of cut at its highest point (use some scrap stock to make practice cuts in order to get the notch correct). Make two passes to cut the notch in each seat support **(See Photo B).** Clean out any roughness in the notches with a chisel if necessary.

❺ Spread exterior, weatherproof glue evenly across the face of the half-lap on one seat support and on the half-lap of a back support. Join the faces, aligning the joint shoulder of each member up tight against the other. Clamp the boards together in position until the glue is dry **(See Photo C).** Glue up all three assemblies.

❻ Use the joined seat support and back support templates to trace an outline of the contours onto the three assembled support structure blanks.

❼ Cut out the support structures with a band saw or a jig saw. Cut carefully along the waste side of the lines **(See Photo D).** File or sand the sawn edges smooth.

8 Rip-cut a piece of 2 × 6 cedar to 3 in. wide on the table saw and cross-cut it to 58½ in. to make the cross support.

9 Enlarge the pattern for the cross support to full size, and transfer it to the workpiece. This will give you the shape of each end and the location of the notches and the eyebolt holes.

10 Cut the seat support notches into the top of the cross support, using your table saw and dado-blade set. Start the end notches 5½ in. in from each end, and center the middle notch. All notches should be 1½ in. wide and 1 in. deep. Cut the notches in at least two passes, using the miter gauge to feed the workpieces (**See Photo E**).

11 With a drill press or a portable drill and a drilling guide, bore a hole through each end of the cross support for the 4-in. eyebolts. Drill from the underside and center the holes 1 in. in from the ends of the board. First, use a ⅞-in. Forstner or brad-point bit to drill ½-in.-deep counterbore holes for the nut and washer. Then drill a ⁷⁄₁₆-in.-dia. guide hole all the way through, locating the drill bit in the centerpoint recess left by the previous bit. To minimize tearout, use scrap wood to back up the exit side (top) when drilling clear through the cross support.

12 Cut the rounded ends of the cross support to shape with a jig saw or coping saw. Smooth the cuts with a sanding block.

13 Set the three L-shaped support structures seat-side down on a flat work surface, so the back support components point toward the floor. Set the cross supports on top of

PHOTO E: Cut 1½-in.-wide notches on the top edge of the cross support. The notches fit together with the notches cut into the bottoms of the seat supports.

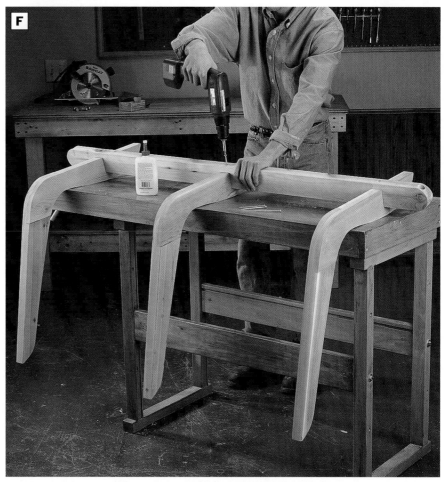

PHOTO F: Attach the support structures to the cross support with weatherproof glue and 3-in. galvanized deck screws. The notches match up to create lap joints.

them, matching up the notches. Drill a countersunk pilot hole at each joint (through the cross support and into each seat support). Attach the parts with waterproof glue and 3-in. galvanized deck screws **(See Photo F).**

INSTALL THE SEAT SLATS

⑭ Rip-cut and cross-cut 16, 2½ × 48-in. slats from cedar stock. We used 1 × 6 in. × 8-ft. boards (¾ in. thick actual).

⑮ Drill three countersunk screw holes into each slat. Clamp two scrap boards (a long and a short) in a right angle to create a reference fence in order to place the holes quickly and consistently **(See Photo G).** Measure from the corner, where the end of each slat will be, and mark off the distances of the three holes. The holes in the slats should be centered on the support structures, so you can get your distances by measuring the support assembly. Place each slat into the fence setup. Hold it tightly against the side and end fences and drill centered holes aligned with the marks on the fences.

⑯ Round over the top edges of each slat with a router and a ¼-in. piloted roundover bit.

⑰ Beginning at the front of the seat support, attach the slats with 2-in. galvanized deck screws. Butt the first three slats up against one another. From there, use a ¼-in. spacers between the slats **(See Photo H).** The ends of the seat slats should be flush with the sides of the supports.

MAKE & ATTACH THE ARMS

⑱ From 2 × 8 cedar stock, rip-cut and cross-cut two arm blanks to 3 × 24½ in., and cut two arm supports to 3 in. × 12⅝ in.

⑲ Make full-size templates for the arms and arm supports, using the *Grid drawings* on page 100 as a reference. Use the templates to trace the appropriate shapes onto the corresponding workpieces. Mark the centerpoints for screw holes and the locations for the bolt holes on the arms.

⑳ Cut the parts out with a band saw or jig saw and smooth the edges and surfaces.

㉑ Drill ⁷⁄₁₆-in.-dia. guide holes with ⅞ in. dia. × ½ in. deep counterbores into the back, outside edge of each arm. The edge of each counterbore should be 1 in. back from the end of the arm **(See Photo I).**

PHOTO G: Drill countersunk screw holes into the seat slats. Use a fence setup with measured guide marks for quick and consistent drilling.

PHOTO H: Screw the slats to the back-and-seat support structures. Butt the first three slats together, then use a ¼-in.-thick spacer between the rest of the slats for consistent gaps. Keep the ends of the slats flush with the sides of the supports.

㉒ Set the table saw blade to 7° and use the miter gauge to cut a bevel on the top (wide) end of each arm support.

㉓ Position the arm supports against the faces of the cross supports, flush with the bottom of the cross supports and with the 7° bevels sloping from front to back. Clamp the arm supports in this position. Attach the arm supports with 2½-in. galvanized deck screws driven through countersunk pilot holes in the arm supports, and into the cross support.

㉔ Attach the arms: Rest each arm on the arm support so the screw hole centerpoints in the top of the arm are centered on the top of the arm support. Hold each arm against the outer back support, and extend the 7/16-in.-dia. guide hole through the back support **(See Photo J).**

㉕ Drill 7/8-in.-dia., ½-in.-deep counterbores on the inside faces of the back supports. Insert a 3/8-in.-dia. × 4-in.-long eyebolt into each arm and through the back support. Thread a nut and washer onto the other end and snug with a wrench. Attach the arms to the arms supports with two 3-in. deck screws driven at the centerpoint locations.

Finishing touches
㉖ Insert 4-in. eyebolts into the counterbored holes in the cross support. Thread nuts and washers onto them and tighten them with a wrench.

㉗ Apply a finish, then hang the swing with heavy rope or chain attached to the eyebolts. Be sure to anchor the ropes or chains with eyebolts into a ceiling joist that can bear the overall weight.

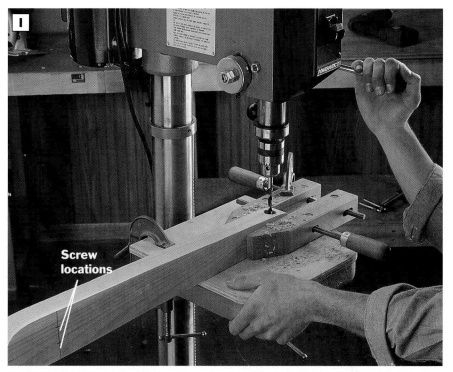

PHOTO I: Use a drill press with a Forstner or brad-point bit to drill counterbored guide holes in edges of the arms for the eyebolts.

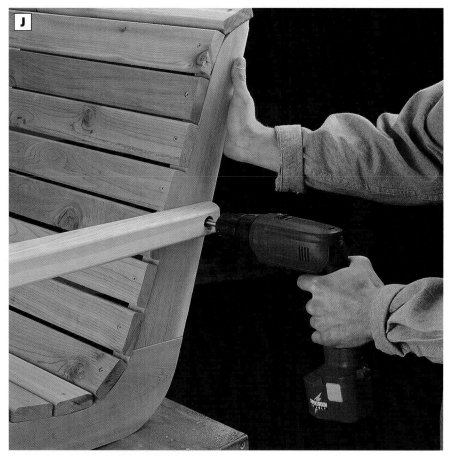

PHOTO J: Extend the 7/16-in. eyebolt guide holes in the arms through the back supports, then attach the eyebolts with washers and nuts.

Kitchen Table

Finding a table that fits into the cramped confines of a kitchen, yet offers generous seating and a sense of style, is a real challenge. Instead of spending countless weekends wandering through furniture stores or tearing through catalogs, build your own kitchen table. The simple round table shown here seats four but doesn't completely consume the room. We built this table with a solid edge-glued tabletop, but to save time and money you can substitute maple veneer plywood with edge banding.

Vital Statistics: Kitchen Table

TYPE: Round table

OVERALL SIZE: 42 in. dia. by 31H

MATERIAL: Hard maple

JOINERY: Dowel joints

CONSTRUCTION DETAILS:

· 42-in.-dia. round tabletop made from seven edge-glued 1 × 6 boards
· Square legs tapered on four sides, with decorative kerfing at the top and bottom
· Tabletop attached with wood buttons
· Seats four comfortably

FINISHING OPTIONS: Two coats of polyurethane on the legs and apron, three coats of gloss polyurethane on the tabletop for an easy-to-clean, water-resistant finish. Use light to medium wood stain for more formal kitchens.

Building time

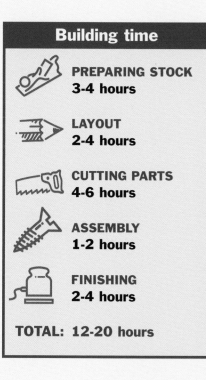

PREPARING STOCK
3-4 hours

LAYOUT
2-4 hours

CUTTING PARTS
4-6 hours

ASSEMBLY
1-2 hours

FINISHING
2-4 hours

TOTAL: 12-20 hours

Tools you'll use

· Table saw
· Jointer or jointing plane
· Surface planer or hand plane
· Router with ½-in. shank and single-fluted straight bit
· Router circle-cutting compass
· Drill/driver
· Tape measure
· 48 in. or longer bar or pipe clamps (6)
· Metal dowel points
· Taper-cutting jig (See page 112)
· Belt sander

Shopping list

☐ (4) 5/4 × 6 in.+ × 8 ft. hard maple boards
☐ (6) 4/4 × 4 in. × 8 ft. hard maple boards
☐ #4 × 3/4 in. flathead wood screws
☐ Biscuits
☐ Wood glue
☐ Finishing materials

Kitchen Table

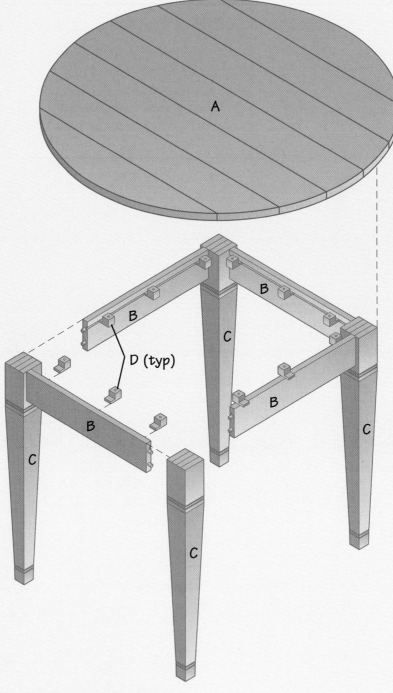

Kitchen Table Cutting List			
Part	**No.**	**Size**	**Material**
A. Tabletop	1	1 × 42 × 42 in.	Hard maple
B. Aprons	4	¾ × 4 × 20 in.	"
C. Legs	4	3 × 3 × 30 in.	"
D. Buttons	12	1 × 1 × 1¾ in.	"

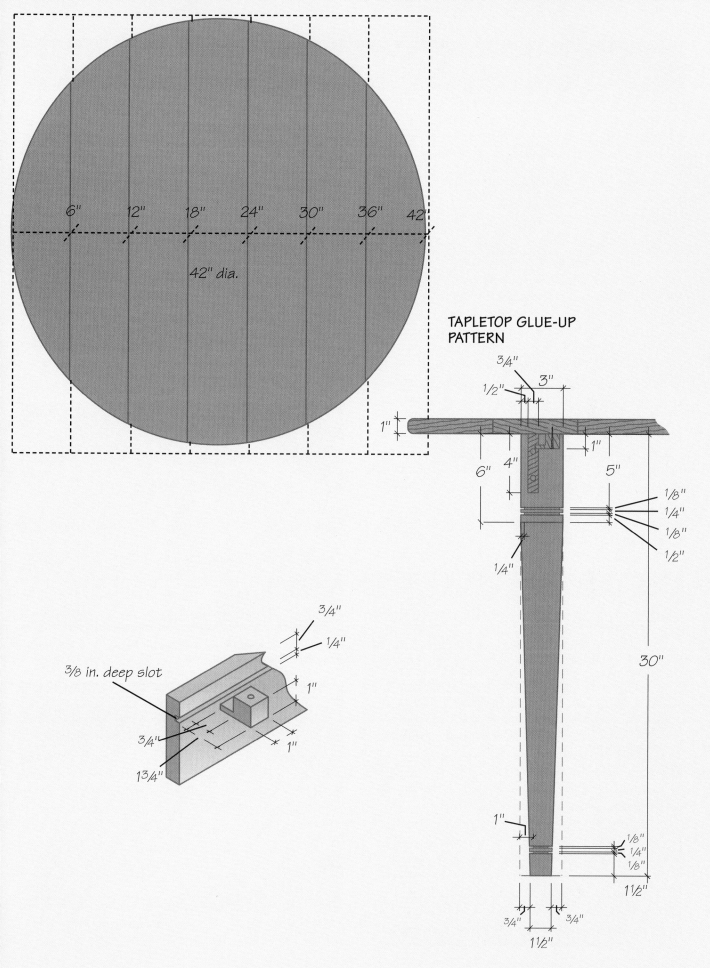

6"   12"   18"   24"   30"   36"   42"

42" dia.

TAPLETOP GLUE-UP
PATTERN

3/4"

1/2"   3"

1"

1"

6"   4"   5"

1/8"
1/4"
1/8"
1/2"

1/4"

30"

3/4"

1/4"

3/8 in. deep slot

1"

3/4"

13/4"   1"

1"

1/8"
1/4"
1/8"

1 1/2"

3/4"   3/4"

1 1/2"

MAKE THE TABLETOP

The round tabletop for this kitchen table is made from 5/4 stock, planed down to 1 in. and edge-glued into a square panel roughly 44 × 44 in. When gluing up a panel, especially for a tabletop, it's best to use an odd number of boards to avoid having a prominent glue-line in the center. You should also use boards of equal width whenever possible. For this panel we used seven 6-in.-wide boards for the glue-up.

1 Starting with 5/4 lumber, joint and plane seven boards just enough to flatten and straighten them, removing as little material as possible. All the boards should be planed to the same thickness. Rip-cut the boards and carefully joint the edges straight and square to yield a 6-in. width, then cross-cut to a rough length of 44 in.

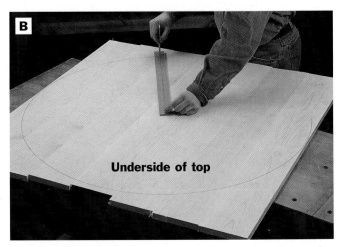

PHOTO A: Cut biscuit slots (or drill dowel holes) in mating edges to keep the boards of the tabletop aligned during glue-up.

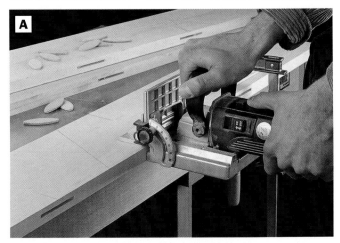

PHOTO B: Draw the outline of the circular tabletop using a homemade trammel created for a 21-in. radius.

PHOTO C: Attach a circle compass to your router to cut out the tabletop. Make several passes of progressively deeper cuts.

CIRCLE-CUTTING WITH A ROUTER

This easy-to-use router jig simplifies cutting perfect circles, from 8 in. up to 48 in. in diameter. The clear plastic arm is attached to your router and replaces the original router base. Some jigs require drilling a hole in your workpiece for the pivot point. The type shown here, however, has a small, sharp brad point that you push into the wood. For best results, use a single-fluted, straight router bit with a ½-in. shank. Set the adjustable locking knob to the radius of your circle, measured from the cutting edge of the router bit. Lock the knob down firmly, drive the pivot pin securely at your centerpoint, and rotate the router counterclockwise around the circle. Cut the circle in several passes, especially in hardwood, gradually lowering the bit after each pass to keep the bit from overheating.

2 Before edge-gluing the boards, lay them out on a flat surface in the order you desire and rough-in a 42-in.-dia. circle. Draw six or seven evenly spaced, parallel reference lines perpendicular to the joints, and number the boards in sequence. Lay out and cut biscuit slots with a biscuit joiner **(See Photo A)**, or drill dowel holes with a doweling jig, using the reference lines as guides, and making sure the biscuits are no closer than 2 in. to the circular cutting line. Glue and clamp the top in sections (don't try to glue up all boards at once), using pipe clamps and wood cauls to protect the edges.

3 After the glue has cured, mark a centerpoint on the underside of the panel. Make a trammel from a 2 × 24-in. hardboard scrap. Drive a finish nail through the trammel at one end, then measure 21 in. out from the point of the nail and mark a drilling point. Drill a ⅛-in.-dia. hole at the point and insert a pencil point. Position the trammel so the point of the nail is secure at the centerpoint of the glue-up and pivot the trammel around the nail to draw your 42-in.-dia. cutting line **(See Photo B).**

4 Attach a circle compass to your router base, set the compass for a 21-in. radius, and insert the pivot pin at the centerpoint of the panel. Install a single-fluted straight bit in the router, then cut the shape in progressively deeper cuts **(See Photo C).**

5 Since the tabletop is too wide to fit in most planers, smooth and flatten the top and bottom surfaces of the tabletop with a hand plane or a belt sander.

6 Install a ⅜-in. piloted roundover bit in the router and round over the profile on both the top and bottom edges of the tabletop.

MAKE THE LEGS
The legs are cut from face-glued boards trimmed to 3 in. square, then tapered on all four sides.

7 Surface-plane six ¼ × 4 × 8 ft. maple boards so they're smooth on both faces and ¾ in. thick. Cut three 31-in. pieces from five of the boards, and one 31-in. piece from the sixth board (the aprons will be cut from the rest of the sixth board). Face-glue groups of four boards **(See Photo D).**

8 After the glue has cured, joint and rip-cut the blanks to 3-in. square **(See Photo E),** then cross-cut them to a length of 30 in.

PHOTO D: Use C-clamps and clamp pads to glue up the leg laminations. Space clamps about 6 in. apart, and protect your worksurface from glue squeeze-out.

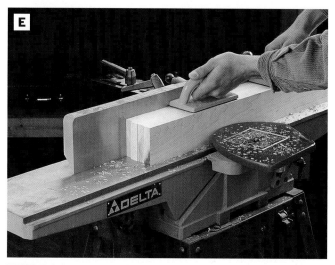

PHOTO E: Joint one edge of each glued leg blank; then rip-cut each blank to 3 in. Make sure the jointed edge rides against the rip fence.

PHOTO F: For a decorative effect, make parallel kerf cuts on the table saw. Use the miter gauge to keep the cuts square.

Tapering jig

PHOTO G: Taper each leg face. If using a purchased tapering jig, follow the manufacturer's directions and safety precautions carefully.

TAPERING JIGS

This product is an improvement on a homemade jig. It's infinitely adjustable from 0° to 15° and has a graduated scale that reads in inches per foot of taper, as well as in degrees. You set the desired taper and lock down the wing nut. Then position one edge of your wooden part against the jig so its end rests against the support clip. Adjust the table saw's rip fence for proper distance (you'll need to do a few trial cuts on scrap wood to determine this). Slide the whole jig along as shown, running one edge along the rip fence and holding the wood tight against the other edge and the clip. Double the taper amount on the third and fourth face to compensate for the removed material.

9 We cut decorative kerfs in the top and bottom of each leg, using a table saw. This is easier to do while the blank is still square (before the tapers are cut). For the top kerfs, set the blade to ¼ in. cutting depth. Using the miter gauge, carefully cross-cut a kerf into all four faces, 5 in. down from the top of each leg. Make a parallel kerf cut, leaving a ¼-in.-wide strip of wood between the kerfs. At the bottom of each leg, set the blade to 1 in. cutting depth and make a kerf cut on all four faces, 1½ in. up from the bottom. Make a parallel kerf cut ¼ in. closer to the top of each leg **(See Photo F).**

10 We used a commercial tapering jig—available in most woodworking stores and catalogs—to cut the tapers in the legs (for more on using a tapering jig, see *Tapering Jigs,* above). The faces of the legs in this table taper ¾ in. over 24 in., starting 6 in. down from the top of the leg. This results in legs that are 3 in. square at the top, and 1½ in. square at the bottom. Cut the tapers on your table saw **(See Photo G).** Make a few practice cuts on scrap stock first.

BUILD THE TABLE BASE

The table base consists of four 20-in. apron boards connected to the tops of the legs with dowel joints. Each apron board has a slot near the top of the inside face for the lips of the wood buttons used to attach the tabletop to the base.

11 Cut the four 20-in.-long aprons; then set the table saw blade to ⅜ in. cutting depth and rip a ¼-in.-wide slot along the top inside edge of each apron. The tops of the slots should be ¾ in. down from the tops of the aprons. You'll need to make more than one pass to achieve the ¼-in.-wide slot.

12 Drill centered guide holes for two ⅜-in. dowels into both ends of each apron. Make sure to avoid drilling into the slots. Use a combination square to draw reference lines for the aprons on adjoining faces of each leg, ½ in. in from the fronts of the legs. Insert metal dowel points into each dowel hole and press the aprons against the tops of the legs so the tops of the aprons are flush with the tops of the legs and the outside faces of the aprons are aligned with the reference lines. Drill perpendicular guide holes at the dowel-point marks **(See Photo H).**

13 Clamp and glue the legs and two of the aprons into two, two-legged assemblies, making sure the legs are square to the apron. After the glue has cured, join the assemblies with the two remaining aprons, completing the table base **(See Photo I).**

ATTACH THE TABLETOP

We used L-shaped wood buttons we made in the shop to attach the tabletop to the table aprons. This allows the wood to expand and contract seasonally without buckling or cracking the joints. The buttons fit into

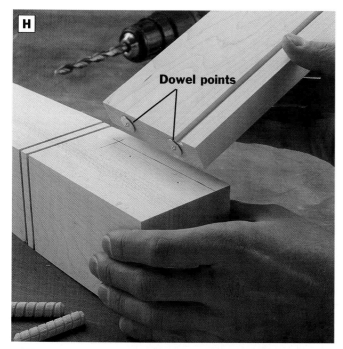

PHOTO H: Metal dowel points will transfer the exact location of the dowel guide holes in this apron end to the surface of the leg.

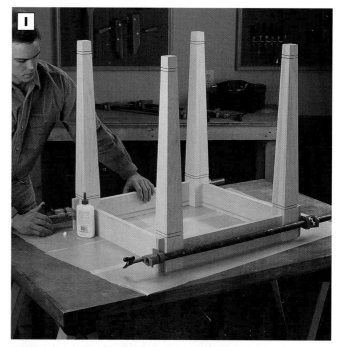

PHOTO I: Assemble the table base in two stages. Above, the two completed leg/apron assemblies are being joined with aprons.

the slots on the insides of the aprons and are screwed to the underside of the tabletop. For this table, you'll need 12 buttons.

⑭ Cut a ¾ × ¾-in. rabbet on the edge of a piece of 1 in.-thick wood (we used a cutoff piece from the tabletop glue-up). Rip the board to 1¾ in. wide and use a ruler and a square to mark off 1-in-long segments. Drill a countersunk pilot hole for a #6 × ¾ in. wood screw in each section, then trim off the 1-in.-wide strips to make the buttons **(See Photo J)**.

⑮ With a sanding block and medium paper (150-grit), round over the edges of the decorative kerf cuts on the legs. Finish-sand all parts to 220-grit and ease all sharp edges. Apply finishing materials to all parts. We used golden maple wood stain and three coats of polyurethane varnish. You may want to apply a couple of extra coats of poly to the tabletop surface for greater durability.

⑯ Set the finished tabletop upside-down on a flat, cushioned surface. Center the frame on the underside of the tabletop, then screw the top to the aprons with three wood buttons attached to each side. Slip the tabs of the buttons into the grooves on the aprons and drive a screw into each countersunk hole **(See Photo K)**. On the aprons that are parallel to the grain of the top, only insert the tabs of the buttons halfway into the grooves to allow for expansion.

PHOTO J: A hand saw is safer than a power saw for trimming wood buttons from the machined hardwood strip.

PHOTO K: With the table base centered on the underside of the tabletop, drive ¾-in screws through each button and into the tabletop.

Tavern Mirror

This tavern-style entry hall mirror makes a dramatic statement to anyone who visits your home. Beyond simply offering practical conveniences, like somewhere to hang a coat and take a moment to fix your hair, it conveys a sense of warmth and welcome. If you're looking for a highly useful woodworking project with low materials cost and high visibility, this tavern mirror is the project for you.

Vital Statistics: Tavern Mirror

TYPE: Entry mirror/coatrack

OVERALL SIZE: 39W by 26H

MATERIAL: Red oak

JOINERY: Dowel joints throughout

CONSTRUCTION DETAILS:
- Arc on top rail and decorative chamfers on inside edges of rails and stiles
- Coved profile on top cap
- Three brass coat hooks
- ¼-in.-thick mirrored glass
- Mounts to wall with screws and lower hanging strip

FINISHING OPTIONS: Use clear topcoat only for more contemporary settings or use medium to dark wood stain for a more traditional wood tone.

Building time

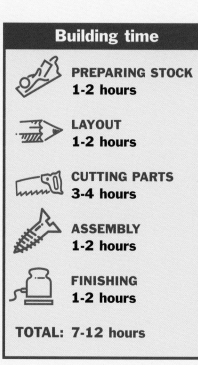

PREPARING STOCK
1-2 hours

LAYOUT
1-2 hours

CUTTING PARTS
3-4 hours

ASSEMBLY
1-2 hours

FINISHING
1-2 hours

TOTAL: 7-12 hours

Tools you'll use

- Router with chamfer and cove bits
- Table saw
- C-clamps
- 42 in. or longer bar or pipe clamps (2)
- Band saw or jig saw
- Combination square
- Doweling jig
- Drill/driver
- Miter saw
- Electronic stud finder

Shopping list

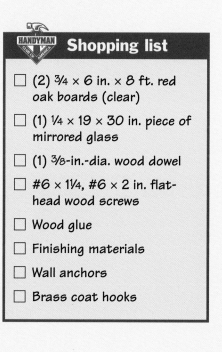

- ☐ (2) ¾ × 6 in. × 8 ft. red oak boards (clear)
- ☐ (1) ¼ × 19 × 30 in. piece of mirrored glass
- ☐ (1) ⅜-in.-dia. wood dowel
- ☐ #6 × 1¼, #6 × 2 in. flat-head wood screws
- ☐ Wood glue
- ☐ Finishing materials
- ☐ Wall anchors
- ☐ Brass coat hooks

Tavern Mirror

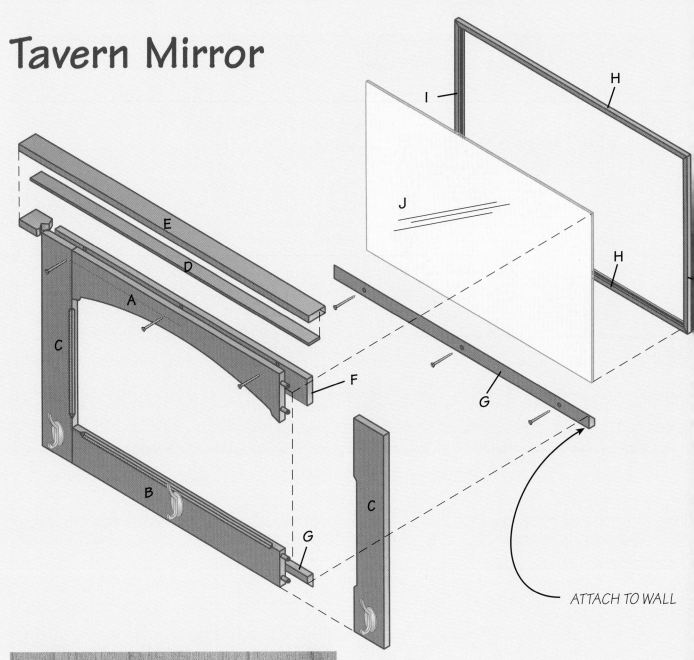

Tavern Mirror Cutting List				
Part	**No.**	**Size**	**Material**
A. Top rail	1	¾ × 5½ × 28 in.	Red oak
B. Lower rail	1	¾ × 4 × 28 in.	"
C. Stiles	2	¾ × 4 × 24 in.	"
D. Coved cap	1	¾ × 1½ × 37½ in.	"
E. Cap strip	1	¾ × 2¼ × 39 in.	"
F. Hang strip (top)	1	¾ × 3 × 34 in.	"
G. Hang strip (lower)	2	¾ × 1½ × 34 in.	"
H. Retainers (top/bottom)	2	½ × ¾ × 31 in.	"
I. Retainers (side)	2	½ × ¾ × 20 in.	"
J. Mirror	1	¼ × 19 × 30 in.	Mirrored glass

ATTACH TO WALL

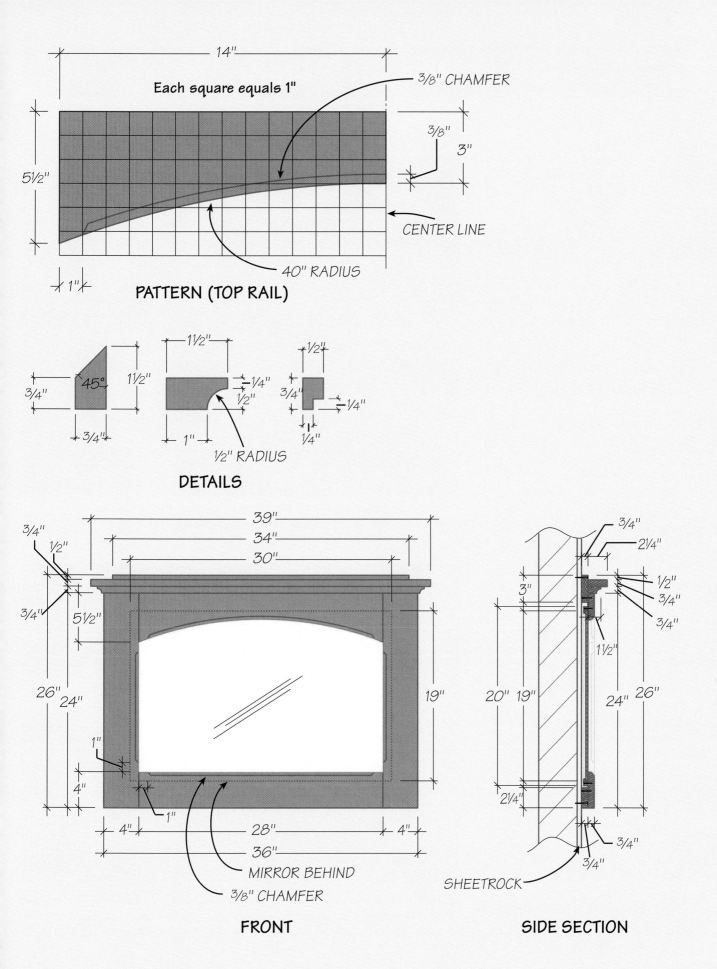

Each square equals 1"

14"

3/8" CHAMFER

3/8"

3"

5½"

CENTER LINE

40" RADIUS

1"

PATTERN (TOP RAIL)

45°

1½"

3/4"

1½"

3/4"

3/4"

1½"

¼"

½"

1"

½" RADIUS

½"

3/4"

¼"

¼"

¼"

DETAILS

39"

34"

30"

3/4"

½"

3/4"

5½"

26"

24"

19"

1"

4"

1"

4"

28"

4"

36"

MIRROR BEHIND

3/8" CHAMFER

FRONT

3/4"

2¼"

3"

½"

3/4"

3/4"

1½"

20"

19"

24"

26"

2¼"

3/4"

3/4"

SHEETROCK

SIDE SECTION

MAKE THE FRAME

The rails and stiles that make up the mirror frame are shaped and profiled prior to assembly.

1 Rip-cut and cross-cut the rails and stiles to size from ¾-in. stock.

2 Enlarge the half-pattern for the top rail curve (See *Grid drawing,* page 117) to full size. Transfer it to ¼-in. scrap hardboard and cut out the shape. Use this half-template to trace the arc onto the top rail, starting at one end and flipping it over to complete the other half of the shape.

3 Cut out the shape with a band saw, jig saw or scroll saw. Smooth the sawn edge with sandpaper or a file.

4 Install a piloted chamfer bit in your router and adjust the cutter height to give a ⅜-in.-deep chamfer (See *Sidebar article,* next page). Rout chamfers along the inside front edges of all the rails and stiles, starting and stopping the cuts at the points shown in the *Front* diagram on page 117 **(See Photo A).**

5 Lay out and drill holes for dowel joints in the rails and stiles using a doweling jig. Biscuit joints may be substituted for dowel joints if you prefer.

PHOTO A: Make decorative stopped chamfer cuts on the inside edges of the rails and stiles. Use a router and piloted chamfer bit to make the cuts. Clamp stopblocks to the rails and stiles to start and stop the router at the proper points.

PHOTO B: Glue up the joints in the rails and stiles and assemble the mirror frame. Clamp, using scrapwood blocks to protect the wood. You can use either dowels or biscuits to help align and reinforce the joint.

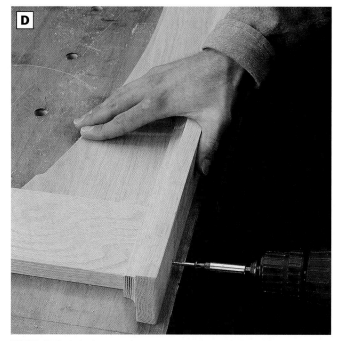

PHOTO C: Rout a coved profile around the front edge and the ends of the cove cap. The workpiece should be at least 3 in. wide to support the router base. Rip it to width after the profiles are cut.

PHOTO D: Attach the two-piece cap assembly to the top of the mirror frame with wood screws and glue.

ROUTER WITH CHAMFER BIT

An easy way to get a consistent chamfer along the edge of a board is to use a router and a piloted chamfer bit. Typical chamfer bits have a 45° angle. Set the router base on the face of the board and run the free-spinning pilot bearing against the board's edge. The distance the cutter protrudes past the router's subbase determines the depth of the chamfer. Adjust the height as close as possible to your desired depth, then make some practice cuts and adjust up or down as needed.

ROUTER WITH COVE BIT

A cove bit is the opposite of a roundover bit: it scoops out a cove, or concave arc, into the edge of a board. Like a roundover bit, cove bits are available with cutters of different radii. As with the chamfer bit, adjust the cutter height to make your desired cut, and run the pilot bearing against the board's edge. Orient the router so the direction of the bit rotation feeds the cutters toward and into the oncoming wood.

6 Apply glue to the mating frame piece ends and to the ends of ⅜ in. hardwood dowels, then clamp the frame assembly together with bar or pipe clamps **(See Photo B).** Make sure the outer edges of the parts are flush.

MAKE THE CAP PIECES
The cap for the mirror frame is a two-piece assembly that spans across the top of the entire frame. The lower cap piece is shaped with a decorative cove, using a router and cove bit.

7 Rip-cut and cross-cut the cap strip to size. Rip-cut the coved cap to 3 in. wide (slightly oversized to leave bearing surface for the router foot), and cross-cut it to 37½ in.

8 Install a piloted ½-in. cove bit in your router (See *Sidebar article,* left). Adjust the cutter height and cut a ½-in.-deep cove **(See Photo C)**, as shown in the illustration on page 117. Rout the ends

PHOTO E: Miter-cut the retainers to length to form a frame around your mirror. We used a power miter saw to make the miter cuts.

PHOTO F: Center the mirror over the back of the frame opening, then frame it with the retainers to hold it in place.

PHOTO G: Bevel-rip a 45° angle on one edge of each lower hang strip, using your table saw and a pushstick and featherboard.

of the coved cap, as well as the front edge, for a three-sided profile. Rip-cut the coved cap to 1½ in. wide.

9 Finish-sand the surfaces of the cap boards, as well as the rails and stiles. Ease all sharp edges with sandpaper.

ATTACH THE CAP PIECES

10 Glue and clamp the coved cap to the cap strip, making sure the back edges are aligned and the cap strip overhangs the ends of the coved cap by an equal amount on each end.

11 Set the cap assembly onto the top rail, flush with the back edge and centered along the length, from end to end. Attach the assembly to the top of the mirror frame with #6 × 2-in. flathead wood screws driven into countersunk pilot holes **(See Photo D).** Use four evenly spaced screws.

INSTALL THE MIRROR

The mirror is held in place with a retainer frame made from ½-in.-thick stock. The retainers are rabbeted on the inside edges to create a reveal for the mirror, then they're screwed to the back of the mirror frame. The ¼-in.-thick mirrored glass can be purchased cut-to-size from any glass store or most hardware stores.

12 On the edge of two ¾-in. oak boards at least 54 in. long, cut a ¼- × ¼-in. rabbet groove (make multiple passes on your table saw with the blade height set at ¼ in., using a rip fence and pushstick). Plane the boards down to a thickness of ½ in., being sure to remove the stock from the non-rabbeted face. Crosscut the retainer frame pieces from these strips, making each piece an inch or two longer than called for in the *Cutting list* on page 116.

13 Miter-cut the retainers to form a frame for your mirror **(See Photo E).**

14 Touch up any rough spots on the front of the mirror frame with sandpaper. Because it's important to finish all of the wood surfaces, we stained and top-coated all frame pieces before installing the mirror. We used a dark walnut-colored stain and tung oil topcoat. Let the finish dry fully before installing the mirror.

⑮ With the mirror frame face-down on a flat surface, center the mirror over the frame opening. Drill countersunk pilot holes for #6 × 1 in. wood screws in the retainer frame pieces, then arrange the retainer frame pieces around the mirror. Secure the mirror by driving screws through the retainers and into the back of the mirror frame **(See Photo F).**

HANG THE MIRROR

The mirror is attached to a wall using a hang strip on top that is screwed to the wall framing members. A beveled hang strip mounted to the bottom of the mirror frame, on the back side, slips over another beveled strip that's mounted to the wall (the standard technique used to hang wall cabinets).

⑯ Cut the hang strips to size. The two lower hang strips are bevel-ripped at a 45° angle along one edge **(See Photo G).** Apply a finish to the top hang strip, then attach it and one of the lower strips to the back of the frame with #6 × 1¼-in. wood screws **(See Photo H).** The top strip should protrude above the top of the frame cap by ½ in. to allow room for driving screws through the strip and into the wall. The bevel on the bottom strip should be facing downward so that its bevel will interlock with the lower strip mounted on the wall. Situate the lower strips such that the other strip (mounted to the wall) will be flush with the bottom edge of the frame.

⑰ Screw the lower wall-mounted hang strip to the wall. Make sure it's level and at the correct height so the center of the mirror is at eye level. Drive screws through the hang strip and into wall framing member locations.

⑱ Before mounting the mirror to the wall, drill pilot holes and screw the coat hooks into the lower frame rail. Take care to position the hooks so they're evenly spaced and aligned horizontally.

⑲ Drill three evenly spaced countersunk pilot holes into the exposed front edge of the top hang strip. Set the mirror frame onto the lower hang strip mounted on the wall **(See Photo I),** then mark the wall anchor locations for screws to affix the upper hang strip. Take the frame down and install wall anchors at the screw locations. Set the mirror back onto the wall strip and attach the top hang strip to the wall. If you're concerned that the screwheads will be visible, cover them with wood putty or use brass screws.

PHOTO H: Attach the top and bottom hang strips to the back of the mirror frame with wood screws driven into counterbored pilot holes.

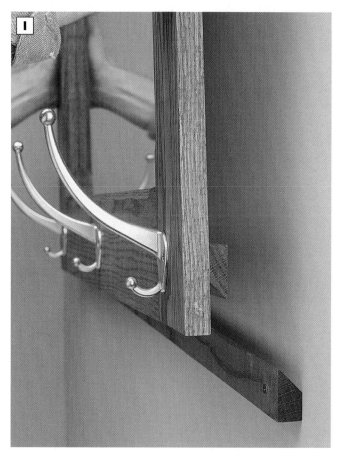

PHOTO I: Attach one lower hang strip to the wall, bevel up, at the desired height of the bottom of the mirror. Use 2 in. or longer screws driven at wall framing member locations. Set the mirror on the strip and mark drilling locations for attaching the top hang strip.

Three-legged Stool

If you've always been intrigued by the wood lathe, but haven't had much experience working with one, this three-legged stool presents an excellent opportunity do some basic spindle turning and faceplate turning, and end up with a useful, traditional piece of household furniture as well. An age-old American design, this stool is a handy aid around the kitchen, bedroom or bathroom, and it makes a great gift for children.

Vital Statistics: Three-legged Stool

TYPE: Small step stool or child's stool

OVERALL SIZE: 12½D by 10H

MATERIAL: Cherry

JOINERY: Mortise-and-tenon (round)

CONSTRUCTION DETAILS:
- Profiled legs spindle-turned on lathe
- Scooped seat, face-plate turned on lathe
- Sanding and finishing of parts completed while parts are mounted in lathe
- Sturdy, 1½-in.-thick seat

FINISHING OPTIONS: Danish oil (or other oil-based top-coat) burnished to rich gloss on lathe.

Building time

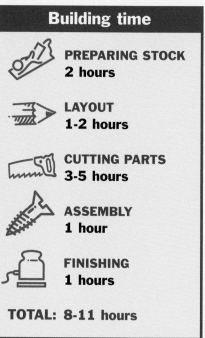

PREPARING STOCK
2 hours

LAYOUT
1-2 hours

CUTTING PARTS
3-5 hours

ASSEMBLY
1 hour

FINISHING
1 hours

TOTAL: 8-11 hours

Tools you'll use

- Table saw
- Planer
- Jointer
- Drill press
- Lathe
- Band saw
- Lathe tools
- 16-in. or longer bar or pipe clamps (2)
- Dovetail or back saw
- Wood mallet
- Center-finder
- Drill/driver
- Power sander

Shopping list

- ☐ (1) 8/4 × 8/4 × 52 in. cherry stock
- ☐ (1) 8/4 × 6½ × 25+ in. cherry stock
- ☐ #8 × 1-in. wood screws
- ☐ Wood glue
- ☐ Finishing materials

Three-legged Stool

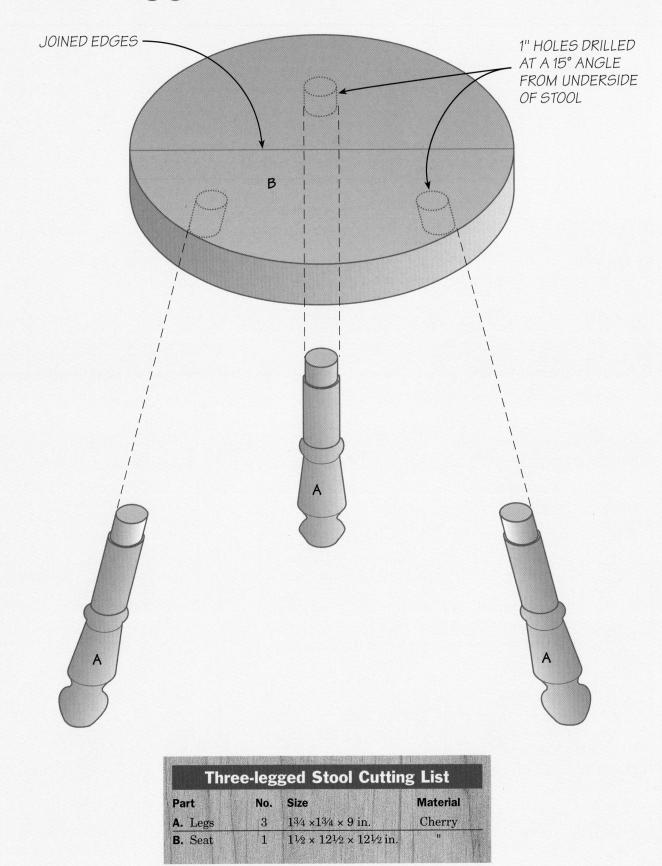

JOINED EDGES

1" HOLES DRILLED AT A 15° ANGLE FROM UNDERSIDE OF STOOL

B

A

A

A

Three-legged Stool Cutting List

Part	No.	Size	Material
A. Legs	3	1¾ × 1¾ × 9 in.	Cherry
B. Seat	1	1½ × 12½ × 12½ in.	"

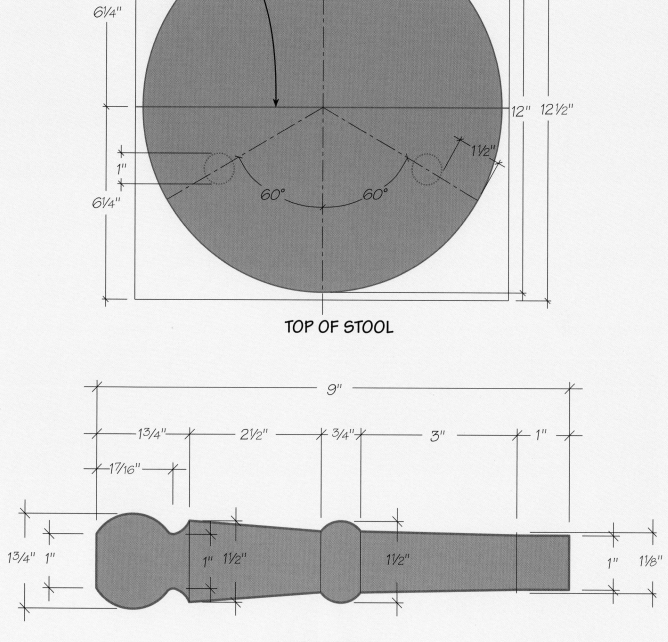

1" HOLES DRILLED
AT A 15° ANGLE
FROM UNDERSIDE
OF STOOL

12½"

BLANK

JOINED
EDGES

1½"

6¼"

12"   12½"

1"

1½"

6¼"

60°   60°

TOP OF STOOL

9"

1¾"   2½"   ¾"   3"   1"

1⁷/₁₆"

1¾" 1"   1" 1½"   1½"   1" 1⅛"

LEG PATTERN

SPINDLE-TURN THE LEGS

❶ Prepare the blanks for turning the stool legs. You'll want a little extra material in both width and length to allow you to mount the spindles on your lathe, and to create a little margin for error when you start turning the shapes. Cross-cut some 2-in.-square cherry to 13-in. lengths to make the leg blanks. In order to have the blank spin true on the lathe, the pointed spindle centers must be mounted into the exact centerpoints of the blank's ends. Find the centerpoints of each end of the blank by drawing diagonal lines connecting the corners (this assumes that the blanks are square to start with). The intersection point is the center. A center-finder makes locating centers easy and quick, and it works for round (cylindrical) stock as well as for square stock **(See Photo A).**

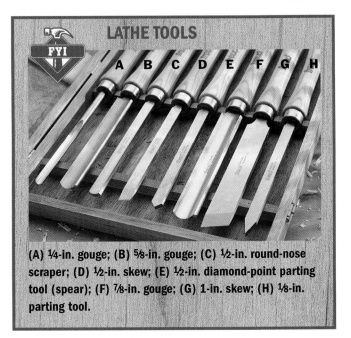

LATHE TOOLS

(A) ¼-in. gouge; (B) ⅝-in. gouge; (C) ½-in. round-nose scraper; (D) ½-in. skew; (E) ½-in. diamond-point parting tool (spear); (F) ⅞-in. gouge; (G) 1-in. skew; (H) ⅛-in. parting tool.

❷ Mount a blank. To save time and effort roughing the blank into a cylindrical shape with the gouge, trim off the edges of all three blanks on the table saw with the blade tilted to 45° (or use a band saw with a 45° wedge beneath each blank). Punch a pilot indentation at the centerpoint of each blank to func-

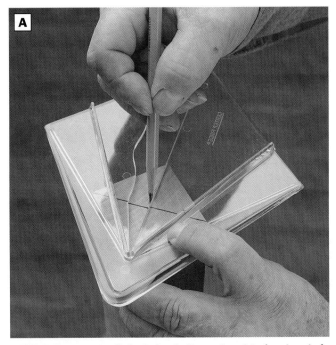

PHOTO A: Use a center-finder to locate the centerpoint of each end of the blank (or simply draw diagonals between corners).

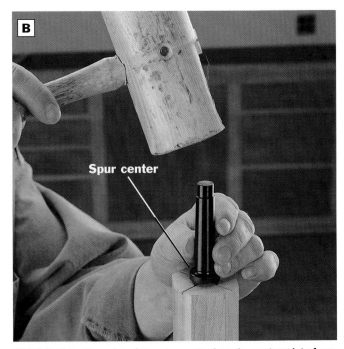

Spur center

PHOTO B: Drive the point of the spur center into the centerpoint of one end of the blank. Test to make sure it is securely bedded.

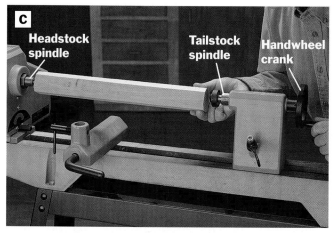

PHOTO C: Mount the spindle in the lathe by fitting the punch point in the free end of the blank over the pointed center in the tailstock spindle, then inserting the spur center into the headstock. Use the handwheel crank to move the tailstock toward the headstock until the blank is held securely in place (but not immobilized).

PHOTO D: Adjust the tool rest so the top edge is roughly even with the center of the blank. The gap between the tool rest and the blank should be no more than ¼ in.

PHOTO E: Trim the octagonal blank into a cylindrical shape with a roughing gouge. Trim the area in front of the tool rest to roughly the planned diameter of the cylinder, then shift the tool rest over and trim the next section in line.

tion as a positive locator for the spindle centers. The end that will be mounted to the headstock will be attached to a spur center, so use a back saw or band saw to cut two shallow kerfs at right angles through the centerpoint of one end. Align the point of the spur center over the centerpoint on the blank's end, then rap the end of the spur center with a wooden mallet (don't use a hammer) to seat the spur center **(See Photo B).** Install a pointed center on the tailstock spindle. Mount the shank of the spur center into the headstock spindle and support the other end of the leg blank with your hand as you move the tailstock up so its spindle center is almost touching the free end of the blank. Lock the tailstock down. Then use the handwheel to crank the tailstock forward until the point of the center inserts into the pilot hole in the blank, and continue cranking until the blank is held snugly between the two spindle centers **(See Photo C).** *Note: If you're using a dead center (one that does not rotate) on your tailstock spindle, lubricate its contact point with the wood using a drop of machine oil or paste wax.*

❸ Position the tool rest. Slide the tool rest's base over until one end of the tool rest extends just past the live area of the blank (where the leg will start). Lock the base and adjust the tool rest so its top edge is slightly below the centerline of the leg blank, and no more than ¼ in. away **(See Photo D).** Lock the tool rest and spin the blank by hand to make sure it clears the tool rest at all points.

❹ Rough-in the leg: Use a ⅞-in. or 1-in. roughing gouge to rough-in a cylinder slightly larger than

PHOTO E: Use a wide skew to scrape the blank until it's a perfect cylinder shape, then smooth out the surface of cylinder by scraping with the skew. Adjust the tool rest as needed so it is no more than ¼ in. from the blank.

PHOTO G: Lay out the pattern for the leg onto the cylinder. Mark the high point and low point of each shape in the profile with a pencil.

PHOTO H: Set the sizing tool to the required diameter of each mark, turn on the lathe, and press down into the blank until the cut has been made to that depth.

1¾ in. dia. (the widest spot on the leg). Turn the lathe on at a fairly slow speed. Hold the handle of the gouge firmly with one hand and grasp the blade with the other hand, near its tip. Keeping the tool angled slightly upward, ease the gouge forward until it contacts the spinning blank. Begin scraping away stock, moving the gouge side to side on the tool rest. To increase the depth of the cut, lift the handle upward slightly. Continue moving the gouge back and forth until you've created a rough cylinder (**See Photo E**), then move the tool rest down the leg and repeat this until the entire blank is roughed in. Stop and move the tool rest forward if the distance to the blank becomes more than ¼ in.

❺ Smooth the spindle. Once the cylinder is roughed in, scrape it with a 1 in. or wider skew to smooth the surface. To prevent gouging, position the skew with the lathe off so that the high point is above the top of the spindle. The blade bevel should be flat with the surface of the spindle. Hold the skew above the spindle, turn on the lathe, and lower the skew until the blade starts to cut. Make light cuts with the skew until the surface of the cylinder is smooth and even all along (**See Photo F**).

❻ Lay out the leg profile. Enlarge or plot out to full size the *Leg pattern* on page 125. Cut out the pattern and affix it to cardboard or hardboard. Cut out the profile of one side to show the outlines of your finished leg spindle. Center the pattern against the leg spindle and make a pencil mark at the edges and top or bottom of each individual shape (**See Photo G**). Then turn on the lathe, and press the pencil against each mark as the leg spins to make full-circle reference marks.

7 Make sizing cuts. The dimensions on the leg pattern tell you the diameters of the low and high points of the shapes on a finished leg. The next step in turning is to cut grooves at these spots on the leg to match those diameters. This will give you reference points to guide you in the shaping step. The sizing cuts are done with a parting tool. To use this tool, simply set it on the tool rest on-edge, align its point with the reference mark on the turning spindle, and gradually press the blade into the spindle until you reach the correct diameter. To achieve the right diameter you can periodically stop and check with calipers. But a handy device called a *sizing tool* makes it a one-step operation. Attach the sizing tool to your parting tool, and set the distance between their tips to the desired diameter. Then lower the sizing tool over the reference line and cut with the parting tool until the correct diameter is achieved (**See Photo H**).

8 Shape the profiles. Now that you have the dimensions of each shape established on the project, cutting the shapes is simply a matter of choosing the right lathe tool and contouring between the the sizing cuts. Beads, coves, grooves, and tapers are the principal shaping cuts made in turning. Remember to always keep the tool angled slightly upward toward the workpiece and keep the tool rest close so the downward-spinning workpiece doesn't catch the tool tip and force it down between the tool rest and the work.
Cutting beads. Beads are convex, rounded rings with shoulders

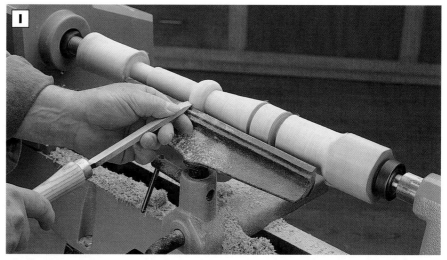

PHOTO I: Shape the beaded portion of the leg by scraping with a small skew or a diamond-point parting tool.

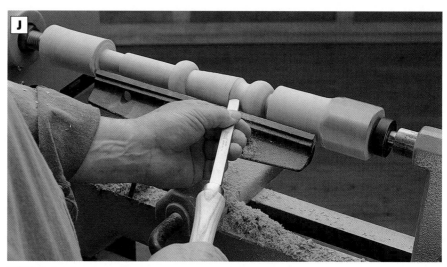

PHOTO J: Cut the coves with a small gouge or a round-nose scraper. Try to get the coves symmetrically shaped on each side of the low point of the cove.

PHOTO K: After all the profiles are shaped, sand the leg smooth while it's still mounted in the lathe. Here, a strip from an old belt-sander belt is being applied to the leg.

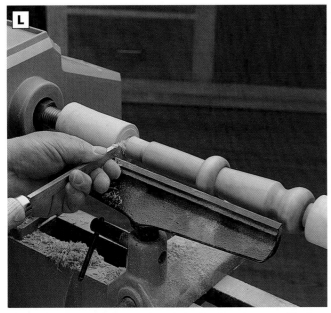

PHOTO L: Cut most of the way through the blank at the top and bottom of the leg, using a parting tool. Be careful not to cut all the way through—the spindle will fly out of the lathe.

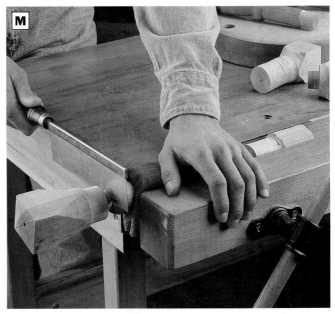

PHOTO M: Dismount the spindle and trim off the ends of the blank using a dovetail saw or any small-tooth hand saw.

nearly perpendicular to the spindle. They can be cut with a small skew or a diamond-point parting tool (also called a spear). Round over the shoulders of the stock between the sizing cuts for each bead, staying as uniform as you can **(See Photo I).**
Cutting coves. Use a small gouge or round-nose scraper to cut these shallow valleys in the spindle **(See Photo J).**
Cutting grooves. Decorative grooves can be cut with several tools. For straight-sided V-grooves, use a skew or a parting tool. For round grooves, use a round-nose scraper or a gouge.
Cutting tapers. Make a series of regularly spaced, increasingly deep sizing cuts, then remove material from between the cuts until the correct thickness is achieved and the taper is well blended.

❾ Sand and finish. Sanding a spindle to prepare for a finish, and even applying the finish, are done easily while the spindle is still mounted in the lathe. With the lathe spinning at its slowest speed, hold strips of cloth-backed sandpaper (old belt-sander belts work well) against the spindle as it spins **(See Photo K).** Sand in increasingly finer grits. Since you are sanding against the grain, you'll need to progress to a finer grit than usual to avoid sanding scratches. Also apply your finish to the lathe-mounted leg. Wipe the leg free of dust, then dab some rub-on finish onto a small cloth and hold it against the spinning work, moving from side to side. We used Danish oil. Don't put finish on the tenons at the top of the leg.

❿ Part the spindle. To remove the leg, cut it to length at each end with a parting tool **(See Photo L).** Stop the cut with about ½ in. or so to go, remove the leg spindle from the lathe, and finish cutting off the waste ends with a sharp hand saw **(See Photo M).**

MAKE THE SEAT
The seat for this three-legged stool is made by edge-gluing two pieces of 6/4 cherry, then cutting the glue-up into a round shape and face-plate turning the blank on the lathe.

⓫ Prepare the blank. Mill two boards to 1½ in. thick and cut them to 6¼ in. wide × 12½ in. long, with one edge of each board jointed square to the faces. Edge-glue the boards with the jointed edges together, keeping the faces and edges aligned. Then plane the blank, if needed, so it's smooth on both faces.

⓬ Lay out the seat. On the underside of the seat, use a straightedge to draw diagonal lines connecting the corners. With the intersection of the lines as a centerpoint, draw a 6¼-in. radius (12½-in. dia.) circle on the blank with a compass. To lay out the leg lines, divide the circle into thirds. Half of one diagonal line (just to the centerpoint) can be one, and use a protractor and straightedge to lay out the other two lines at 120° angles from it (or 60° from the other half of the diagonal). Mark the centerpoints of the leg holes by measuring 2 in. in from the perimeter of the circle along the lines. Then use a compass to draw

PHOTO N: Lay out the critical location marks (centerpoint, leg holes and seat perimeter) on the underside of the seat blank.

PHOTO O: Mount the faceplate so it's exactly centered on the blank. A large piece of wood like this rotating off center is difficult to handle.

PHOTO P: Carefully turn the edge to a round shape with a gouge, removing small amounts of wood at a time.

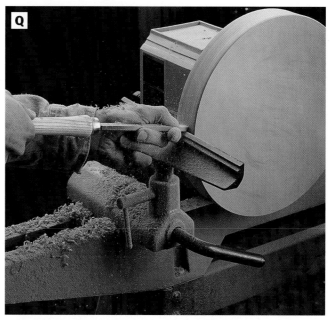

PHOTO Q: Smooth the edges of the seat with a round-nose scraper. Note that the scraper is angled down so it will scrape, not cut.

½-in.-radius (1-in.-dia.) circles from these points **(See Photo N)**.

⓭ Cut out the blank. Cut just to the waste side of the perimeter line with a band saw or a jig saw.

⓮ Attach the face plate. To accurately center the faceplate, draw a circle on the blank the same diameter as the faceplate, using a compass with its point stuck in the blank's center mark. Attach the blank with #8 × 1-in. wood screws **(See Photo O)**.

⓯ Turn the outside to a round shape: Attach the faceplate to the headstock—either on the outside spindle or, if your headstock rotates, turn it to the side to allow clearance for the large seat blank. Set the tool rest at about the center line of the blank, and roughly ⅛ in. away from its edge. Use a strong ⅞-in. gouge and a slow speed (300 to 500 rpm for roughing this diameter workpiece). Present the tool carefully to the work, handle down. Remove very little wood with each cut, and as you rotate the blade back and forth across the edge of the wood don't let

PHOTO R: Turn a gentle, shallow cup in the face of the seat with a round-nose scraper.

PHOTO S: Smooth the surface of the stool seat with the flat edge of a parting tool.

PHOTO T: Use a random-orbit sander to sand the seat smooth. Be sure to turn off and unplug the lathe first.

PHOTO U: Let the seat revolve on the lathe while you rub on your finish. Set the lathe at a slow speed (around 500 to 700 rpm).

the corners of the blade touch the wood or they'll dig in, possibly sending chunks of wood and the gouge itself flying (**See Photo P**).

⓰ Smooth the edge. After the gouge is applied, the surface will still be slightly rough, particularly at the two end grain areas. Smooth the surface with a ½-in. round-nose scraper. Hold the scraper with the handle up, so it scrapes rather than cuts (**See Photo Q**).

⓱ Shape the seat top. Turn a slight cup in the face of the seat with a ½-in. round-nose scraper. Set the tool rest along the left side of the turning, and adjust the height so the scraper will cut at or near the center line. Move the tool along the tool rest to create a gentle curve with a lip at the edge of the seat. Work only on the left half of the turning (**See Photo R**).

⓲ Smooth the surface. Use the flat edge of a diamond-point parting tool to carefully smooth out the tool marks on the face of the seat (**See Photo S**).

⓳ Sand the seat. Remove the tool rest and sand the edge of the seat as the lathe turns, like you did with the legs. Then turn off the lathe and sand the top of the seat with a random orbit sander (**See Photo T**).

⓴ Apply finish. With the lathe rotating, apply the same wipe-on finish you applied to the legs (**See Photo U**).

㉑ Remove the seat from the lathe and fill the screw holes with a matching wood filler.

ASSEMBLE THE STOOL

㉒ Drill the mortises for the round tenons at the tops of the legs. First, install a 1-in. Forstner bit in your drill press. Tilt the drill press table to a 15° angle and clamp the seat to the table so the drill bit is aligned over the top of one of the mortises. Set up for drilling each hole by arranging the seat so the point of the mortise outline closest to the edge of the seat is the highest point of the circle. Set the depth stop so the hole will be 1 in. deep at its shallowest point, then drill each mortise (**See Photo V**).

㉓ Sand the seat bottom to smooth out any tearout from the drill bit. Erase the pencil lines and finish-sand the underside of the seat. Ease the sharp edge.

㉔ Glue in the legs: Apply glue into the mortises and onto the leg tenons and drive the legs into their mor-

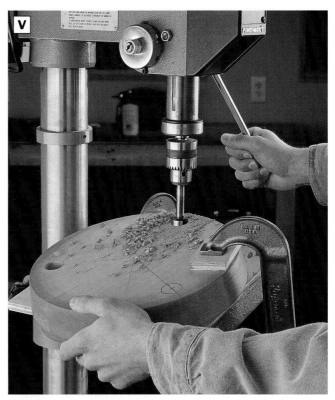

PHOTO V: Drill 1-in.-dia. × 1-in.-deep mortises for the round leg tenons, using a drill press with the table set at a 15° angle.

PHOTO W: Assemble the stool by gluing the leg tenons into the mortises. Drive them in until the shoulders bottom out.

tises until they bottom-out at the tenon shoulders (**See Photo W**).

㉕ Clean off the excess glue around the joints and test to make sure the stool does not wobble when resting on a flat surface. If wobble exists, mark the high leg and sand down the bottom a little at a time until it rests evenly. Apply your finish to the bottom of the stool and to the bottoms of the legs.

Plant Stand

Both practical and attractive, this unique plant stand will brighten up any corner of your house. The ceramic tile top is mounted on a removable tray for easy cleaning or replacement. We used inexpensive Philippine mahogany to build the base, but you can use just about any wood you choose.

Vital Statistics: Plant Stand

TYPE: Plant stand

OVERALL SIZE: 15⅞W by 28H by 15⅞D

MATERIAL: Mahogany

JOINERY: Dowel joints

CONSTRUCTION DETAILS:

· Tile top is mounted to a removable tray so the tile can be cleaned or replaced if it breaks or becomes worn

· Top rails keep objects from sliding off tiled surface

· Decorative chamfers on tops of solid mahogany legs

· Lower shelf functions as a stretcher between legs

FINISHING OPTIONS: Clear coat with tung oil varnish. Paste filler for wood grain is a good option for mahogany. Match wood tones to tile color.

Building time

PREPARING STOCK
1-2 hours

LAYOUT
2-4 hours

CUTTING PARTS
2-4 hours

ASSEMBLY
2-4 hours

FINISHING
1-2 hours

TOTAL: 8-16 hours

Tools you'll use

· Table saw

· Jointer

· Planer

· Router table with piloted chamfering bit

· Tape measure

· 24-in. or longer bar or pipe clamps (6)

· C-clamps

· Spring clamps

· Combination square

· Doweling jig

· Drill/driver

· Back saw or dovetail saw

· Portable drill guide

· Power sander

Shopping list

☐ (2) 1½ × 1½ in. × 6 ft. mahogany (Philippine or Honduras—Philippine is shown here)

☐ (1) ¾ × 8 in. × 8 ft. mahogany

☐ ½-in.-plywood scrap for tray bottom (birch plywood is shown here)

☐ (1) 12 × 12-in. ceramic floor tile (or smaller tiles to create a 12 × 12-in. sheet)

☐ Tile adhesive, grout and penetrating sealer

☐ (1) ⅜-in.-dia.; (1) ¼-in. dia. wood dowel for shelf pins

☐ #6 × 1, 1¼-in. wood screws

☐ Wood glue

☐ Finishing materials

Plant Stand

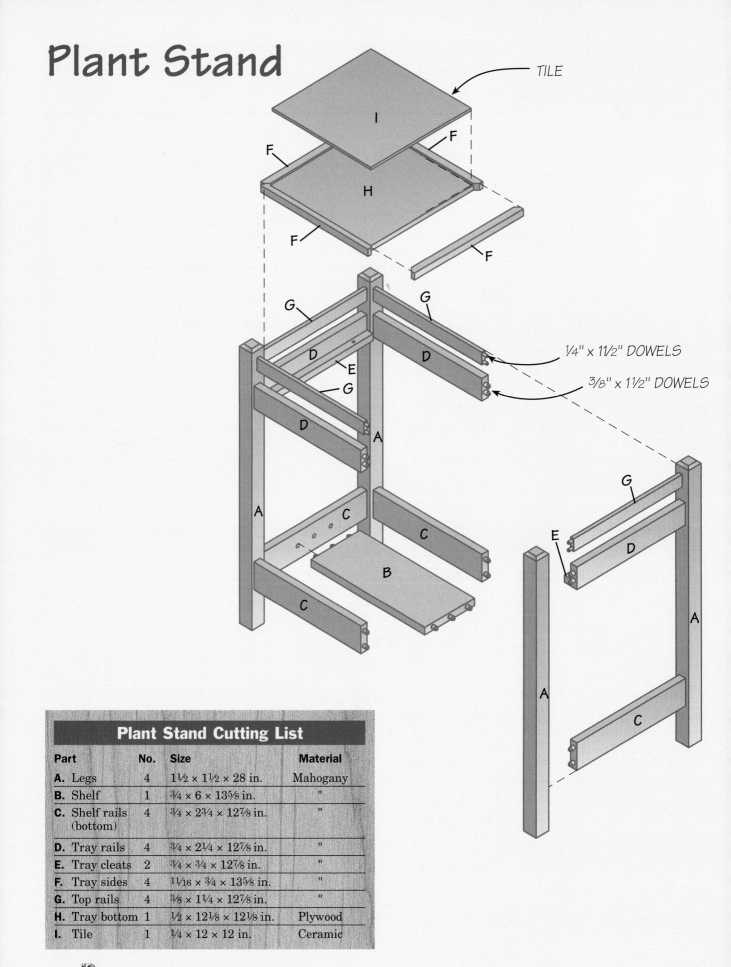

TILE

I

F

F

F

F

H

F

¼" x 1½" DOWELS

⅜" x 1½" DOWELS

G

G

D

D

E

G

A

D

A

C

C

B

C

G

E

D

A

A

C

Plant Stand Cutting List

Part	No.	Size	Material
A. Legs	4	1½ × 1½ × 28 in.	Mahogany
B. Shelf	1	¾ × 6 × 13⅝ in.	"
C. Shelf rails (bottom)	4	¾ × 2¾ × 12⅞ in.	"
D. Tray rails	4	¾ × 2¼ × 12⅞ in.	"
E. Tray cleats	2	¾ × ¾ × 12⅞ in.	"
F. Tray sides	4	11⁄16 × ¾ × 13⅝ in.	"
G. Top rails	4	⅜ × 1¼ × 12⅞ in.	"
H. Tray bottom	1	½ × 12⅛ × 12⅛ in.	Plywood
I. Tile	1	¼ × 12 × 12 in.	Ceramic

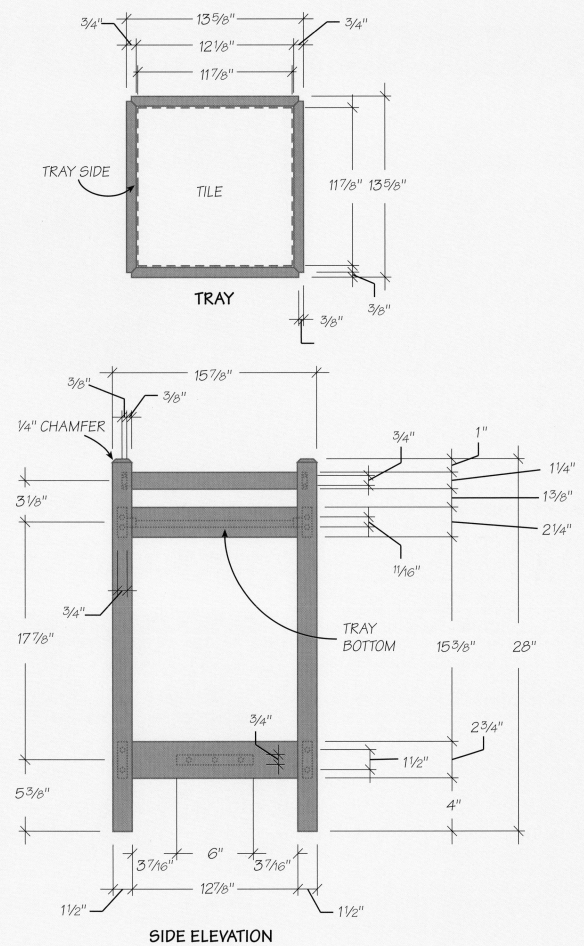

3/4"   13⁵/₈"   3/4"

12¹/₈"

11⁷/₈"

TRAY SIDE

TILE

11⁷/₈"   13⁵/₈"

3/8"

3/8"

TRAY

15⁷/₈"

3/8"   3/8"

¼" CHAMFER

3/4"   1"

1¼"

1³/₈"

2¼"

3¹/₈"

11/16"

3/4"

TRAY BOTTOM

15³/₈"   28"

17⁷/₈"

3/4"

2³/₄"

1½"

5³/₈"

4"

3⁷/₁₆"   6"   3⁷/₁₆"

12⁷/₈"

1½"   1½"

SIDE ELEVATION

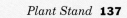

MAKE UP THE PARTS

❶ Joint, plane and rip-cut stock to 1½ × 1½ in. square. Cross-cut the four legs to 28 in. long.

❷ Chamfer the tops of the legs. We used a router table with a chamfering bit, but you could also use a stationary disc sander with a table, or even a small block plane. Set up your tool to cut a ¼-in. chamfer. If using a router table, position a fence with a bit relief cutout so its face is flush with the pilot bearing of the bit. To prevent tearout of the grain on the trailing edge of the cuts, back up each leg with a block of scrapwood as you feed the workpiece over the bit. We used a square pushboard to feed the workpieces and to provide a surface for keeping the backup block tight against the workpiece (**See Photo A**). Chamfer all four edges of each leg top.

❸ From ¾-in. stock, rip-cut and cross-cut the four tray rails, the two bottom shelf rails, and the bottom shelf to size, using the dimensions given in the *Cutting list* on page 136. Then cut the four top rails to size from ⅜-in. stock (either resaw or plane thicker stock to ⅜ in. thick). All 10 rails can be cross-cut together at the same setting (12⅞ in. long). A power miter saw is a good tool for these crosscuts.

ASSEMBLE THE PLANT STAND

❹ Lay out and drill all of the dowel holes to join the rails to the legs. There are two dowels per joint. Refer to the *Illustration* on page 137 for placement. A doweling jig like the one shown in *Photo B* will greatly simplify this work. The dowel joints for the tray rails and the bottom shelf rails are centered on the legs. They require ⅜-in. holes for 1½-in.-long dowels, but the dowel holes are only drilled ½-in. deep into the legs. The ¼-in.-dia. dowel holes in the legs for the top rails are off-center. If you place a ⅜-in.-thick spacer on the inside of the leg before clamp-

PHOTO A: Chamfer the top edges of each leg. A backup block of scrap wood prevents tear-out on the trailing edge of the cut, while a push-board keeps it tight against the workpiece and permits a uniform, safe pass over the cutter and against the fence. Use a wood fence with a bit relief cutout.

PHOTO B: Drill dowel holes in the legs for the top rails. Since these joints are not centered on the legs, use a ⅜-in.-thick spacer to offset the doweling jig the proper amount.

ing the doweling jig to the workpiece, this will shift the centerpoints of the jig holes the correct amount off-center **(See Photo B).**

5 Drill the ⅜-in. dowel holes for attaching the bottom shelf to the bottom shelf rails. Use the same doweling jig to drill the holes into the ends of the shelf (three in each end). To bore the holes in the shelf rails, use a portable drill with a drill guide or a drill press with a brad-point bit **(See Photo C).** Drill only ½ in. deep into the rails.

6 Assemble two sides of the plant stand separately. Glue, dowel and clamp the parts together. For each side assembly, attach one bottom shelf rail, one tray rail, and one top rail between two legs **(See Photo D).** Measure the diagonals from corner to corner to check for square, and adust the clamp pressure as needed until the diagonals are equal.

7 Glue the dowels into the joints and clamp up the two side assemblies and remaining rails to complete the plant stand framework. Be sure to glue and clamp the bottom shelf in place at the same time. This serves as a stretcher to tie the lower legs together, as well as a shelf **(See Photo E).**

8 Rip-cut a ¾ × ¾-in. strip to make the tray cleats, and cross-cut to 12⅞ in. long. Due to the delicateness of parts this small size, the most effective tool to use is a sharp back saw in a miter box.

9 Drill countersunk screw holes for attaching the cleats to the inside faces of two opposing tray rails. Also drill two countersunk screw holes up through the bottom of each cleat for attaching the tray.

10 Apply glue to the tray cleats and use a spring clamp to hold them to the inside faces of tray rails on two opposite sides of the plant stand. The bottom edges of the cleats should show the countersunk ends of the screw holes and should be flush with the bottom edges of the tray rails. Drive #6 × 1¼-in. wood screws through the countersunk screw holes to attach the cleats to the tray rails **(See Photo F).**

ASSEMBLE THE TRAY

11 Cut the ½-in. plywood tray bottom to 12⅛ × 12⅛ in. We used birch plywood sanded on both sides.

12 Make up four tray sides from ¾-in.-thick stock. Rip them to ¾ in. wide. This will limit the depth of

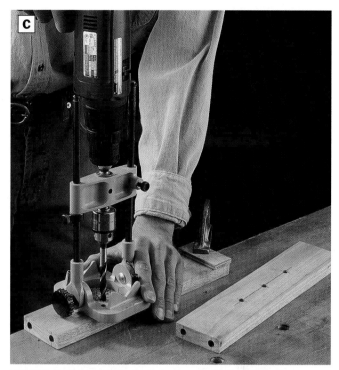

PHOTO C: Drill dowel holes in the bottom shelf rails. We used a portable drill mounted in a portable drill guide equipped with a depth stop. Use a brad-point bit.

PHOTO D: Using dowel joints, glue and clamp up the legs and cross supports on a flat surface. Waxed paper protects your worksurface from glue spillage.

the tray recess so the top surface of the tile will be slightly above the tray sides. Leave the strips oversize in length.

13 Miter-cut the ends of the tray sides so they wrap around the tray bottom with their miters fitting together tightly. This can be done on a table saw with a miter gauge or on a chop saw.

14 Glue and clamp the tray sides to the tray bottom. Apply glue to the miters and to the edges of the plywood. Use scrapwood cauls to distribute the

PHOTO E: Glue up the frame base for the plant stand. Slip wood cauls between the heads of the bar or pipe clamps and the plant stand. Position the cauls so they distribute the clamping pressure evenly across multiple joints, if possible.

PHOTO F: Attach the tray cleats to the inside faces of the tray rails, using glue and #6 × 1¼-in. wood screws. The bottoms of the cleats should be flush with the bottom edges of the tray sides and should feature countersunk screw holes for attaching the tray bottom.

PHOTO G: Glue and clamp the tray sides to the tray bottom, aligning the mitered corners. No additional reinforcement is required.

PHOTO H: Cut ⅜ × ⅜-in. notches in the outside corners of the tray to allow it to fit around the inside corners of the legs. Use a small, fine-tooth saw like the dovetail saw shown above. Make sure to keep the tray plumb as you cut.

clamping pressure and to protect the wood from the clamps **(See Photo G)**. Glue-up the tray on a flat surface, making sure the bottom of the tray bottom and the tray sides are flush.

⑮ After the glue has dried, remove the clamps. Use a combination square to mark out ⅜ × ⅜-in. notches in the mitered corners of the assembled tray to fit around the inside corners of the legs. Use a back saw or dovetail saw to cut out the notches, cutting carefully along the waste sides of the lines **(See Photo H)**.

APPLY FINISHING TOUCHES

⑯ Finish-sand the plant stand and the top surfaces of the tray sides. Ease all exposed sharp edges with sandpaper (but only ease the top, inner edges of the tray sides).

⑰ Apply the wood finish. We used Danish oil. For a fine finish, apply grain filler to the wood first—mahogany responds well to filler.

⑱ After the finish is thoroughly dry, tape off the top surfaces of the tray sides to protect the wood.

⑲ Lay a base of tile adhesive on the tray bottom and set the tile or tiles. See the information on pages 148 to 149 of the *Tile-top Coffee Table* for more information on installing tile.

⑳ Seal the tile and any grout lines with penetrating sealer **(See Photo I)**.

㉑ When the sealer is dry, remove the tape from the wood. Set the finished tray in place on the cleats, and screw it to the cleats from below with #6 × 1-in. flathead wood screws **(See Photo J)**.

PHOTO I: Seal unglazed tile and grout joints with penetrating sealer. Use a disposable foam brush to apply the sealer. Because a plant stand is likely to be exposed to a considerable amount of moisture, sealer is important to protect the plant stand top and to help inhibit mildew and other forms of discoloration that can affect the grout.

PHOTO J: Lay the plant stand on its side and attach the finished tray by driving #6 × 1-in. screws up through the countersunk screw holes in the bottoms of the tray cleats.

Tile-top Coffee Table

High durability and a fresh look are two of the best reasons for choosing to build a table with a ceramic tile tabletop. An increasingly popular design element, tile adds new textures and colors to wood furnishings. When combined with a strong, simple birch table base, the effect is quite stunning—as you can see.

Vital Statistics: Tile-top Coffee Table

TYPE: Coffee table

OVERALL SIZE: 49½L by 15H by 25½D

MATERIAL: Birch with ceramic tile top

JOINERY: Rabbet joints and butt joints reinforced with glue and screws

CONSTRUCTION DETAILS:

· Tabletop is made of 32 ceramic floor tiles applied to an MDF substrate

· Rabbets cut in leg tops create ledges for the aprons

· Hardwood cleats provide support for tabletop

· Counterbores filled with wood plugs

FINISHING OPTIONS: Clear coat for casual, contemporary look enhanced by tiles; alternately, birch can be stained to take on on the characteristics of most other wood species.

Building time

PREPARING STOCK
2 hours

LAYOUT
2 hours

CUTTING PARTS
3-5 hours

ASSEMBLY
2-4 hours

FINISHING
2-4 hours

TOTAL: 11-17 hours

Tools you'll use

· Table saw
· Jointer
· Surface planer
· Cross-cutting saw
· Flush-cutting saw
· Tape measure
· 36-in. or longer bar or pipe clamps (6)
· Wood mallet
· Combination square
· Drill/driver
· Counterbore/countersink bit
· Dado-blade set
· Notched trowel
· Grout float

Shopping list

HANDYMAN CLUB OF AMERICA

☐ (1) 4 × 4 in. × 6 ft. solid birch

☐ (2) ¾ or 4/4 × 4 in. × 8 ft. birch

☐ (2) 1½ × 1½ in. × 8 ft. inexpensive hardwood

☐ (1) ¾ × 24 × 48 in. MDF particleboard

☐ (32) 6 × 6 ceramic floor tiles

☐ Tile adhesive and grout (latex additive optional)

☐ Wood glue

☐ #10 × 2-in. wood screws

☐ ⅜ × ⅜ wood plugs

☐ Finishing materials

Tile-top Coffee Table

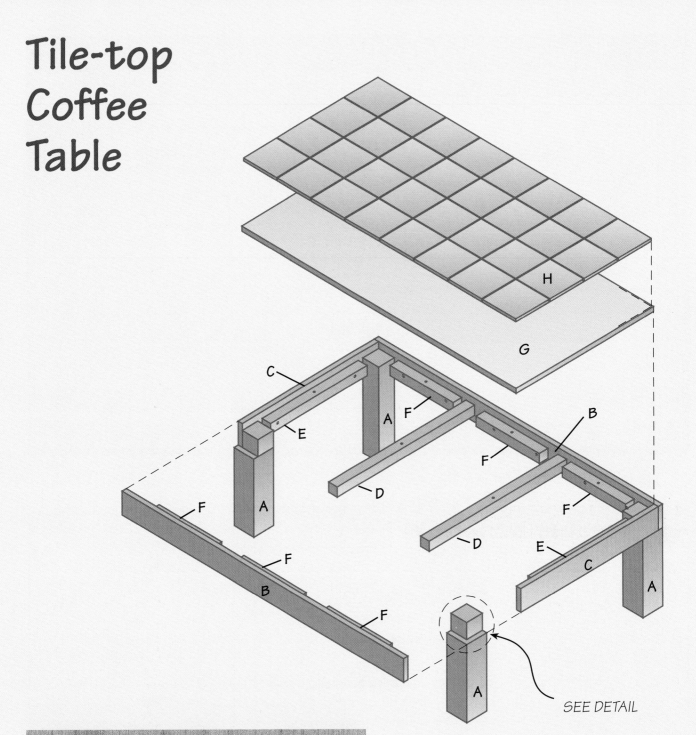

SEE DETAIL

Coffee Table Cutting List			
Part	**No.**	**Size**	**Material**
A. Legs	4	3½ × 3½ × 14 in.	Birch
B. Side Rails	2	¾ × 3½ × 49½ in.	"
C. End Rails	2	¾ × 3½ × 24 in.	"
D. Cleats (middle)	2	1½ × 1½ × 24 in.	Hardwood
E. Cleats (end)	2	1½ × 1½ × 17 in.	"
F. Cleats (side)	6	1½ × 1½ × 11 in.	"
G. Sub-top	1	¾ × 24 × 48 in.	MDF
H. Tiles	32	¼ × 6 × 6 in.	Ceramic

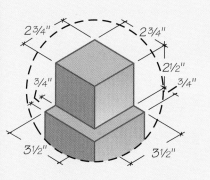

**DETAIL
(TOP OF LEG)**

2¾"   2¾"
¾"   2½"   ¾"
3½"   3½"

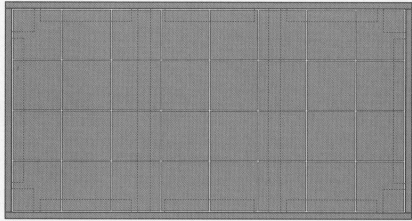

TOP VIEW

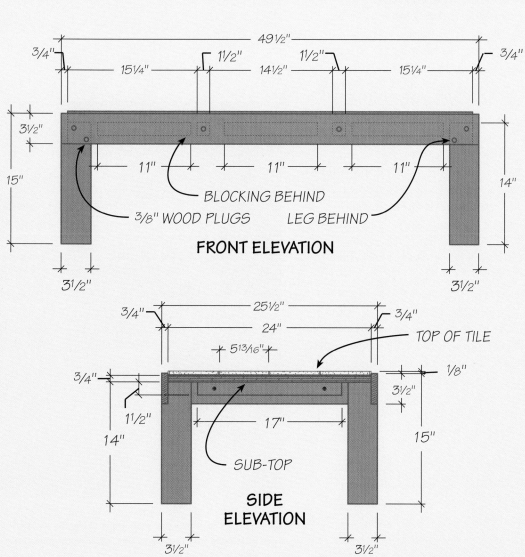

49½"
¾"   1½"   1½"   ¾"
15¼"   14½"   15¼"
3½"
15   11"   11"   11"   14"
BLOCKING BEHIND
⅜" WOOD PLUGS   LEG BEHIND
3½"   3½"

FRONT ELEVATION

25½"
¾"   24"   ¾"
5¹³⁄₁₆"   TOP OF TILE
¾"   1/8"
3½"
14   1½"   17"   15
SUB-TOP
3½"   3½"

**SIDE
ELEVATION**

NOTE: *Because the actual dimensions of tile can vary significantly among styles and manufacturers, we strongly recommend that you purchase the tile for your table before you begin building the table base. A nominal 6 × 6 tile you may find can be anywhere from 5½ to a full 6 in. square. Rather than cutting the tiles to fit, purchase the style and color you like and dry-lay the tiles to the approximate size of the coffee tabletop (24 × 48 in. if you build it as shown here). Measure the width and length of the dry-lay, and base the size of your aprons and substrate on that dimension (don't forget to allow about 1/16 to 1/8 in. between tiles for grout joints if your tiles don't have nibs that set the grout joint automatically).*

PHOTO A: Make rabbet cuts in the tops of two adjoining faces of each leg to create ledges for the rails. We used a dado-blade set. Feed the stock with the miter gauge to assure a square cut.

MAKE THE LEGS

The legs for this coffee table were made from solid 4-in.-thick birch stock. If you're unable to find wood of that thickness, or if you choose to build the coffee table with a different wood species that's not available in such beefy dimensions, simply laminate thinner strips to make the leg stock (See the *Workbench* project, pages 28 to 35).

❶ Joint and plane the leg stock to 3½ in. thick. Ideally, use a workpiece that's at least 58 in. long. To prepare the stock, run two adjoining faces through your jointer to create flat, smooth faces, then rip-cut the stock so it's square and slightly thicker than 3½ in. Reduce the stock to 3½ in. square using a planer or jointer. Cross-cut four lengths to 14 in. long to make the legs.

❷ The legs are rabbeted on the top, outside faces to create ledges for the rails. Lay out the shoulders of the rabbets by drawing square lines on adjoining faces, 2½ in. down from the top of each leg. If you've laminated the legs, mark the cuts so the grain is consistent on each side (i.e., the faces of both legs on a

PHOTO B: Attach the side and end rails to the legs with two screws per joint. Stagger the screws as shown to keep screws on adjoining sides from interfering with each other. The screw hole counterbores will be plugged with wood plugs.

particular side should be either edge grain or face grain when viewed from straight on).

3 We used a dado-blade set mounted in a table saw to remove the stock in the rabbet areas. A band saw can also be used or even a hand saw if you've got some time to kill. Set the dado-blade set for its widest cut, and adjust the cutting height to ¾ in. Use a miter gauge to guide each work-piece across the dado set, starting at the end and working your way toward the shoulder line **(See Photo A).**

MAKE THE RAILS & ASSEMBLE THE TABLE BASE

4 Cut the end rails and side rails to finished size.

5 Lay two legs down on a work-surface, about 4 ft. apart, with the rabbeted sides facing up and out. Place a side rail on top of the legs in the rabbeted recess. Adjust the legs so the outside corners are flush with the ends of the rail and the lower edge of the rail is tight up against the shoulders of the rabbets. Clamp the rail into posi-tion and drill two counterbored pilot holes through the rail into each leg. The counterbore should be ⅜-in.-dia. × ⅜-in.-deep to accept a standard-sized wood plug. Apply glue to the mating surfaces, then drive #10 × 2-in. flathead wood screws into the counterbored pilot holes to attach the rails to the legs. Repeat the procedure for the other side rail and the other two legs, creating two side-rail assemblies.

6 Stand the two sides upright and attach the end rails between the side-rail assemblies **(See Photo B).** Make sure the ends of the end rails are tight against the

PHOTO C: Attach cleats to the rails with glue and screws. Drill countersunk pilot holes in the bottoms of the cleats (for attaching the sub-top) before installing them.

PHOTO D: Drive 2-in. screws through the cleats and into the underside of the sub-top. If your drill/driver has a clutch, set it to a low setting to help avoid overdriving the screws.

inside faces of the side rails.

7 The substrate for the tiled tabletop (we're calling it the "sub-top") will rest on top of the legs, at a point 1 in. down from the top edges of the rails. To support the weight of the substrate and tile, we added cleats that are installed with their tops flush to the tops of

the legs. To mark the cleat loca-tions, draw reference lines all around the inside faces of the rails, 1 in. down from the top.

8 Cut the 10 cleats to length from 1½ × 1½-in. stock (any hard-wood will do). Drill two evenly spaced, countersunk screw holes into one face of each cleat for the

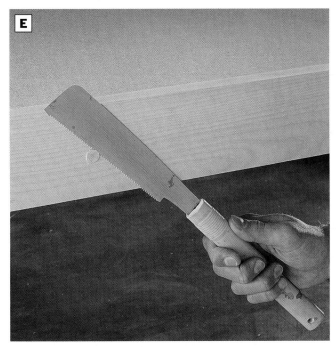

PHOTO E: Plug the screw holes with plugs cut from scraps of the same wood used to make the table base (if you have a plug cutter). When the glue is dry, trim the ends of the plugs with a flush-cutting saw, like this Japanese saw.

PHOTO F: Finish-sand the table base and apply the finish you've chosen. We simply topcoated the wood with three coats of clear Danish oil, preserving the natural color of the wood.

screws that will be used to attach the substrate.

❾ Attach the cleats at the locations shown in the *Grid patterns* on page 145, using glue and 2-in. screws driven into countersunk pilot holes. Make sure the tops of the cleats are aligned with the reference lines **(See Photo C).** The middle cleats are attached with screws driven through counterbored pilot holes in the outside faces of the aprons, and into the ends of the cleats.

❿ Cut the sub-top to size from ¾-in. particleboard or plywood. We used MDF (medium-density fiberboard) particleboard, which is a superior substrate material to either plywood or ordinary oriented-strand particleboard.

⓫ Spread glue on the top surfaces of the cleats. Drop the top in and flip the whole table upside down onto blocking. Drive 2-in.

screws through the cleats and into the sub-top **(See Photo D).**

⓬ Plug the screw counterbore holes. Birch plugs in the standard ⅜ × ⅜-in. size are fairly easy to find. For a better match, cut your own plugs from scrap pieces of your stock, using a plug cutter mounted in your drill press. Apply glue to the ends of the plugs and tap them in with a wood mallet. Trim the ends of the plugs flush with the rails using a flush-cutting hand saw **(See Photo E).**

⓭ Sand the table base with 150-, then 180-grit sandpaper and ease all sharp edges and corners. Apply your finish of choice to the rails and legs (but not the sub-top). We applied a clear Danish oil finish **(See Photo F).**

INSTALL THE TILES

⓮ Tape off the top edges of the rails with masking tape to protect the wood from the tile adhesive.

⓯ Apply tile adhesive to the sub-top. It can be a thinset mortar or mastic. Spread it evenly across the entire surface with a notched trowel **(See Photo G).**

⓰ Set the tiles in the adhesive **(See Photo H).** Don't use too much top pressure when setting the tiles—you could squeeze out all the adhesive from beneath the tiles and ruin the bond. If your tiles are not self-spacing, try to keep even gaps of ¹⁄₁₆ to ⅛ in. on all sides of each tile.

⓱ When the adhesive is fully set (see manufacturer's recommendations), grout the tiles. Choose a grout color that complements the tile color. *TIP: For added resistance to cracking, add latex grout additive to dry grout mix instead of water.* Spread the grout diagonally across the joints with a rubber grout float. Fill all the gaps to the top **(See Photo I).** When the grout has begun to set up, wipe

PHOTO G: Apply a medium-thick layer of tile adhesive (dry-set mortar or mastic) to the surface of the sub-top, using a notched trowel. Protect the finished wood with tape.

PHOTO H: Set the tiles into the bed of adhesive, spacing them evenly so the gaps are consistent. Press down lightly on each tile to seat it into the adhesive, but take care not to apply too much pressure. Leave a gap of about ⅛ in. between the tiles and the tops of the rail boards. Try to get the tiles positioned correctly on the first try, minimizing the need to move and adjust them.

PHOTO I: Spread grout into the joints between tiles (and around the border of the tiled top), using a grout float. Always wear rubber gloves when working with grout. Use a latex additive in the grout to help keep it from crumbling and to improve the bond with the tiles.

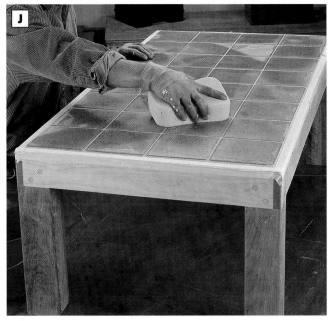

PHOTO J: Before the grout dries completely, wipe off the excess from the surfaces of the tile, using a damp sponge. After the grout is dried, buff the tile with a soft cloth to give it a glossy sheen.

the excess from the surfaces of the tiles with a damp sponge **(See Photo J).** Continue until the tiles are clean—grout can be very hard to clean off once it dries. Work diagonally across the joints, being careful not to remove grout from between the joints.

⑱ Remove the masking tape from the wood, pulling it up slowly.

Garden Bench

Made from dimensional cedar, this garden bench has a rustic quality that lets it blend into a casual, country-style garden. But the graceful curve of the top rail on the backrest gives this bench just enough style to fit into a formal garden as well. With its sloped back and contoured seat, it offers a comfortable resting spot where you can while away the hours in the great outdoors.

Vital Statistics: Garden Bench

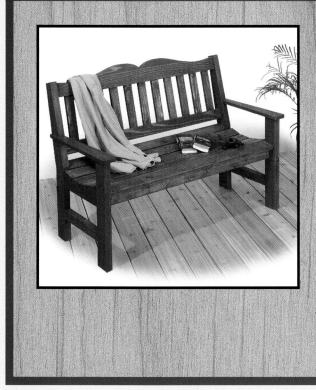

TYPE: Outdoor bench

OVERALL SIZE: 50W by 34H by 24D

MATERIAL: Cedar (1× and 2×)

JOINERY: Dowel joints, butt joints reinforced with screws

CONSTRUCTION DETAILS:
· Sloped back rest and contoured seat for comfort
· All wood parts made from standard dimensional cedar available at building centers
· Decorative contour on top back rail
· Seats three adults

FINISHING OPTIONS: Clear coat UV-inhibiting wood sealant to prevent graying of wood. Apply redwood-tinted stain for richer wood color.

Building time

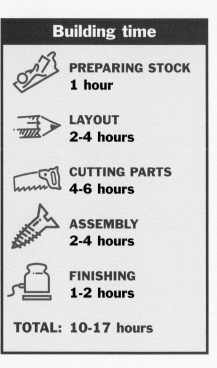

PREPARING STOCK
1 hour

LAYOUT
2-4 hours

CUTTING PARTS
4-6 hours

ASSEMBLY
2-4 hours

FINISHING
1-2 hours

TOTAL: 10-17 hours

Tools you'll use

· Table saw or circular saw
· Drill/driver
· Straightedge cutting guide
· C-clamps
· Bar or pipe clamps
· Jig saw or band saw
· Hammer
· Combination square
· Tape measure
· Doweling jig

Shopping list

☐ (1) 2 × 8 in. × 8 ft. cedar dimension lumber

☐ (1) 2 × 6 in. × 8 ft. cedar dimension lumber

☐ (3) 2 × 4 in. × 8 ft. cedar dimension lumber

☐ (6) 1 × 4 in. × 8 ft. cedar dimension lumber

☐ (60) ¼-in.-dia. × 1½ in. fluted wood dowels

☐ Finishing materials

☐ Galvanized deck screws (2 in. and 3 in.)

☐ Exterior wood glue

Garden Bench

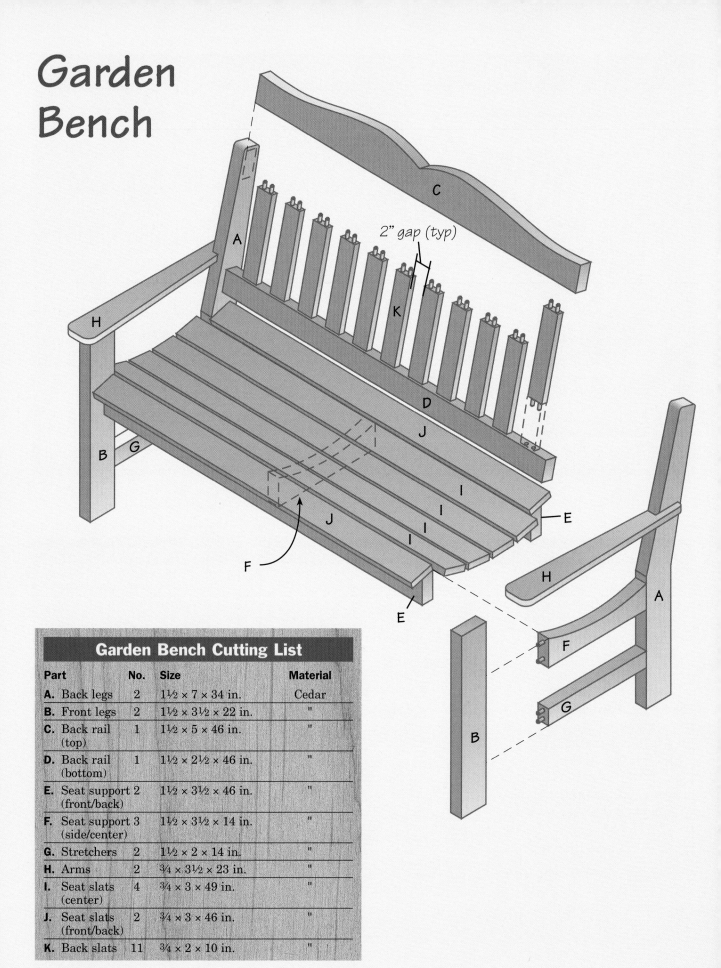

2" gap (typ)

A

B

C

D

E

F

G

H

I

J

K

Garden Bench Cutting List

Part	No.	Size	Material
A. Back legs	2	1½ × 7 × 34 in.	Cedar
B. Front legs	2	1½ × 3½ × 22 in.	"
C. Back rail (top)	1	1½ × 5 × 46 in.	"
D. Back rail (bottom)	1	1½ × 2½ × 46 in.	"
E. Seat support (front/back)	2	1½ × 3½ × 46 in.	"
F. Seat support (side/center)	3	1½ × 3½ × 14 in.	"
G. Stretchers	2	1½ × 2 × 14 in.	"
H. Arms	2	¾ × 3½ × 23 in.	"
I. Seat slats (center)	4	¾ × 3 × 49 in.	"
J. Seat slats (front/back)	2	¾ × 3 × 46 in.	"
K. Back slats	11	¾ × 2 × 10 in.	"

Each square equals 1"

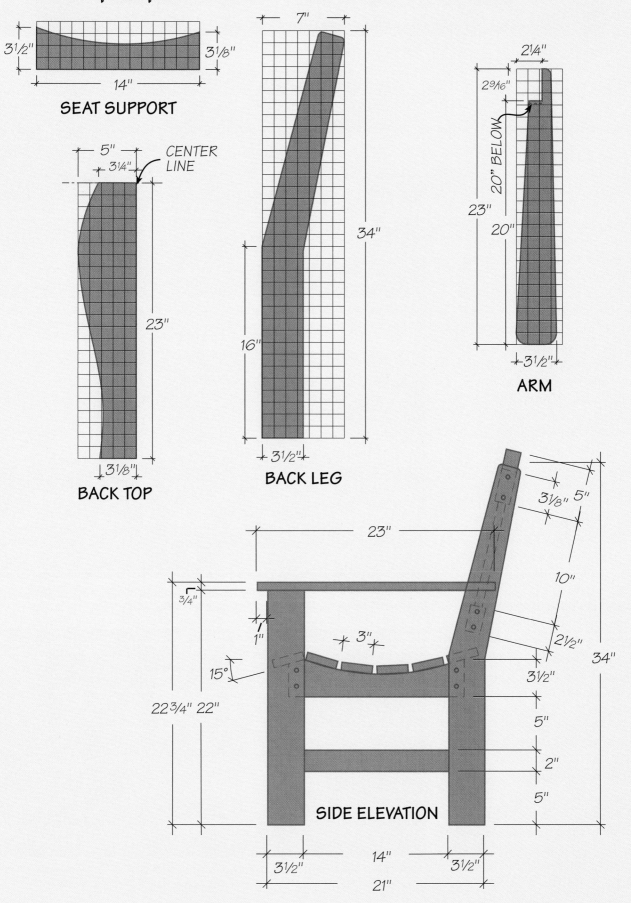

SEAT SUPPORT

3½"   3⅛"
14"

BACK TOP

5"
3¼"
CENTER LINE
23"
3⅛"

BACK LEG

7"
34"
16"
3½"

ARM

2¼"
2⁹⁄₁₆"
20" BELOW
23"
20"
3½"

SIDE ELEVATION

23"
3/4"
1"
15°
3"
3⅛"   5"
10"
2½"
3½"
34"
5"
2"
5"
22¾" 22"
3½"   14"   3½"
21"

Since a garden bench is designed for use outdoors, the wood type options are fairly limited. Cedar and redwood are two exterior woods that traditionally have been cheaper than other wood types suitable for outdoor use, like white oak or teak. But diminishing supply has driven up the price of cedar and redwood in some regions of the country. The most cost-effective wood for building any exterior project is usually pressure-treated pine. The drawbacks are that treated pine doesn't stain well (you'll probably want to paint the project), and it releases dangerous irritants when cut. Wear gloves when handling treated pine, and wear a particle mask when machining it.

CUT THE CONTOURED PARTS

The top back rail, back legs, arms and side/center seat supports all feature contours. The patterns for the shapes can be found on page 153. The pattern for the top back rail is a half pattern. Reverse the template on the centerline shown to draw the other half.

❶ Cut the top back rail, back legs, arms and side/center seat supports to length and width, according to the dimensions in the *Cutting List* on page 152. Transfer the patterns for each part to the workpiece. For the arms, seat sup-

PHOTO A: Cut the contoured bench parts with a jig saw or a band saw. Make sure to transfer the patterns accurately and secure each workpiece to your worksurface if cutting with a jig saw.

PHOTO B: Label the back slats with numbers that correspond to their positions on the top and bottom back rails, then drill dowel holes at each joint using a doweling jig.

PHOTO C: Glue and dowel the back slats into the bottom back rail, then glue the dowels into the dowel holes on the top end of each slat. Glue the dowels into the top rail, then clamp.

PHOTO D: Make sure the bevels on the front and back seat supports are facing up and pointing toward the back of the bench, then attach the center seat support with glue and 3-in. deck screws.

PHOTO E: Make bench side assemblies by joining a front leg to a back leg with a side seat support and a stretcher. Reinforce the glue joints with dowels.

ports and rear legs, draw the pattern on one workpiece only, then use that workpiece as a template for marking the other similar pieces after the part is cut to shape. Cut the contours with a jig saw or band saw (**See Photo A**). Smooth out all cuts with a file or sander. Use a file or a chisel to smooth the top center V-point of the shape. Do not cut out the rear-leg notches on the arms yet.

MAKE THE BACK REST

2 Rip-cut a piece of 1× cedar to 2 in. wide, then cross-cut the eleven 10-in.-long back slats.

3 Lay out all the rails and slats on a flat surface. Allow 2-in. spacing between slats and at the ends (you can cut 2-in. spacer blocks if this will help). Number the slats in sequence and note the numbers on the back rails so you know how the parts go together.

4 Lay out and drill two ¼-in.-dia. × ¾-in.-deep dowel holes at each slat location and in both ends of each slat. We used a doweling jig (**See Photo B**).

5 Finish-sand all the parts of the back with 150-grit sandpaper.

6 Assemble the back, using exterior (moisture-resistant) wood glue. Apply glue to each dowel end and pound the dowels home with a wood mallet (**See Photo C**). Put the parts together and clamp up the assembly. Be careful to pad the clamps so the parts don't get marred. Clean up any squeeze-out and leave the clamps on until the glue sets.

MAKE THE BENCH FRAME

The frame for the garden bench consists of the front and back legs, the seat supports, and the stretchers that fit between the front and back legs near the bottom.

7 Cut the front and back seat supports to size. Set the table saw blade to 15° and rip a bevel along the top edge of each. Finish-sand the front, back, and center seat supports.

8 Mark a centerpoint along the length of each seat support. Measure ¾ in. to each side of the

centerpoint and draw square lines down the faces of the boards. Attach the center seat support on these lines with glue and 3-in. galvanized deck screws (two per joint). Drill clearance holes for the shanks before driving the screws, and make sure the bevels on the tops of the seat supports are both facing up and pointed toward the back of the bench. Use a bar clamp or pipe clamp on each side of the center seat support (**See Photo D**).

9 Cut the two front legs and the two leg stretchers to size. Finish-sand the front and back legs, the stretchers, and the side seat supports.

10 The next step is to put together the two end assemblies. Lay out dowel joints on the front and back legs so the leg stretchers are 5 in. up from the bottom ends, and the side seat supports are 5 in. up from the stretchers. *Note: the shorter ends of the seat supports go against the back legs.*

Brace

12 in.

PHOTO F: Drive 3-in. deck screws through the rear legs and into the ends of the rear and front seat supports to complete the rough assembly of the bench frame. Clamp braces to the front and back seat supports so they stand 12 in. above the worksurface.

PHOTO G: Fit the backrest assembly between the rear legs so it's centered and the top rail of the back rest is ⅜ in. below the tops of the rear legs. Clamp the assembly in position, then attach the backrest by driving 3-in. deck screws through the rear legs and into the rails.

⓫ Mark out and drill two dowel holes per joint. Glue and clamp the front and back legs, the stretchers, and the side seat supports into two pairs (See Photo

E). Use clamp pads to protect the wood.

⓬ Attach one side assembly to the end of the center seat support

assembly. Use glue and two 3-in. deck screws per joint. Drive the screws through the legs and into the ends of the seat supports. (The seat section needs to be held at 12 in. off the floor and level while you're working, so cut four pieces of scrap 2 × 4 to about 16 in. long and clamp them near the ends of the front and back seat supports to hold them at the right height.) Glue and screw the remaining side assembly to the seat section (See Photo F).

INSTALL THE BACK REST
⓭ Mark placement lines for the ends of the backrest assembly on the upper inside faces of the rear legs. The top and bottom rails should be centered on the width of the legs, with the ends of the top rail located ⅜ in. down from the top of the legs.

⓮ Clamp angled scrap support blocks under the back assembly to hold it up at the right height, and start by drilling and screwing the tops of the legs to the top rail— two screws per joint. Then check for alignment, and drill and screw through the legs into the bottom rail (See Photo G).

ATTACH THE SEAT SLATS
⓯ Rip-cut the six ¾-in.-thick seat slats to 3 in. wide. Cross-cut the four center slats to 49 in. long and the front and back slats to 46 in. Finish-sand all the slats.

⓰ Glue and screw the front and back seat slats to the front and back seat supports. Use 2-in. deck screws. Align the inside edges of the slats with the inside edges of the seat support bevels. Use one screw near each end and a third screw in the center (so it will line up with the screws attaching the slats to the center seat support).

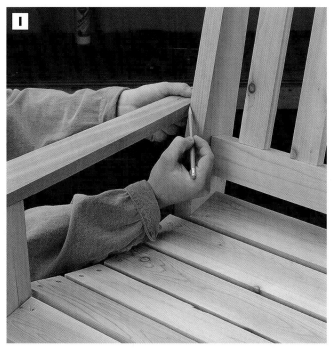

PHOTO H: Attach the seat slats to the seat supports by driving one 2-in. deck screw through each slat at the ends and at the center of slat. Use ½-in. spacers to set the distance between the slats.

PHOTO I: The arms are notched to fit around the rear legs. After laying out the notches, set each arm in position and trace the line of the rear leg onto the arm to mark the cutting angle for the front of the notch.

17 Screw the center seat slats to the side and center seat supports. Butt the first one up to the front seat slat, and use ½-in. spacers between the others to ensure even gaps. The ends of the center seat slats should be flush with the side seat supports. Use one screw per joint **(See Photo H).**

ATTACH THE ARMS

18 Mark cutting lines for a notch in the back of each arm where it will meet a rear leg (See *Grid Pattern,* page 153). Position each arm so it's centered on the front leg and the front cutting line of the notch aligns with the front edge of the rear leg. Make sure the arm is level. Mark the angle of the front of the rear leg onto the edge of the arm **(See Photo I).** Mark both arms, then use a small back saw or a dovetail saw to cut out the notches (make sure to follow the bevel at the front of each notch).

19 Attach the arms to the front legs with glue and 2-in. deck screws **(See Photo J).** At the rear leg joints, drive the screws through the outside edges of the arms and into the rear legs.

APPLY FINISHING TOUCHES

20 Touch up any remaining rough surfaces with sandpaper and ease all sharp edges. Apply the exterior finish of your choice, or leave the bench to weather naturally to a rustic silver-gray.

PHOTO J: Attach the arms to the tops of the front legs with 2-in. deck screws driven into countersunk pilot holes in the arms. Use two screws per joint. Attach the arms to the rear legs by driving screws through the side edges of the arms and into the rear legs. Glue all joints.

Index

Index of Projects